COLLECTING
MALT WHISKY
A PRICE GUIDE

COLLECTING MALT WHISKY

A PRICE GUIDE

SECOND EDITION

MARTIN GREEN

GREEN BLAKE ENTERPRISES LIMITED

First published in 2007 by
Green Blake Enterprises Limited
Bloomsbank
Auchincruive
Ayr
KA6 5HT

ISBN: 978-0-9555266-0-2

British Library Cataloguing-in-Publication Data
A catalogue record for this book is available
from the British Library

Typeset by Mark Blackadder

Special thanks to:

Glen Moore, Bowmore

David Cox, The Macallan

Jason Craig, Highland Park

Neil MacDonald, Aberlour

Hamish Torrie, Ardbeg

Chris Rigby, The Balvenie

David Robertson, Dalmore

Brian Clements, McTear's

Richard Joynson, Loch Fyne Whiskies

Richard Parker, Parker's Whisky

Keir Sword, Royal Mile Whiskies

Mackenzie Baird, The Whisky Mouse

Donald and Alistair Hart, Hart Brothers

Wayne Ormerod, whisky-online.com

Mark Blackadder, page make-up and design

Printed and bound by Blackmore Ltd, Shaftesbury, Dorset SP7 8PX

Introduction

I am delighted to be able to present the second edition of Collecting Malt Whisky and wish to thank the contributers for ther valued support.

The data printed in this publication is empirical and covers six years of auction results at McTear's Fine and Rare Whisky Auctions. The figures printed are actual hammer prices and even though multiple lots have been divided appropriately, when cataloguing, I generally try to make lots up of bottles of similar value thus ensuring that when I calculate the average hammer price, the figure is a fair representation. Buyers premium has not been added to the figures published.

Generally speaking, all bottles that come under the hammer at auction are in good condition, with good labels, good levels and good seals, however where the condition is poor, for any reason, I have stated this.

The majority of bottlings listed in this publication were bottled by the distillers themselves, however independent bottlings have the company name in brackets after the entry, the majority being: (Adelphi), (Blackadder), (Cadenhead's), (G & M, Gordon & MacPhail), (Hart Brothers), (Douglas Laing), (Murray McDavid), (SMWS, Scotch Malt Whisky Society), etc.

The first whisky to come under the hammer in Glasgow was sold at auction in 1986. These sales have been built up over a twenty year period as of June 2006. The City of Glasgow has been the International Auction Centre for whisky since 1986. At that time, my then boss sent me on a house call to look at some whisky and vintage wine since he either couldn't be bothered or was too busy to attend himself, I remember thinking that whisky being sold at auction had possibilites and how true the case it has proved to have been. The first dedicated auction took place in 1989, previously whisky was included in a section of a Fine Wine Auction, by 1995 the annual auctions became a bi-annual event and since joining forces with McTear's in 2000 the collectors market has driven the auctions forward to four each year, in March, June, September and December.

There are many factors which have contributed to the existence of whisky auctions; first and foremost The Scotch Whisky Industry itself. The range of bottlings, past and present, that have been released onto the market are vast, the history and heritage of the Industries' bottlings continue to inspire the Collector and build the Industries' future in the field of collecting. The more recent expressions and releases, controlled at the discretion of the Industry may become the liquid art of the future.

In my opinion as long as the Scotch Whisky Industry continues to release rare bottlings, the market will continue to develop and expand. Over the past two decades I have witnessed a growing demand for rare and collectable whisky, however it is worth noting that to view the hobby of collecting malt whisky as an investment one should think in the long term. Rare whisky like any other precious and collectable commodity is susceptible to the laws of supply and demand. Therefore we must treat it like any other investment, which is speculative. There is always an element of risk. Whisky does however have that added bonus – you can always drink it. The effects of 9/11 were evident on the auction market, however from 2003 onwards the market began to recover, more noticably from 2005 onwards.

In my experience, those people who have benefited most from their investment in whisky have treated it as a long term plan, perhaps reaping their rewards from it ten years or so later.

What makes whisky collectable is the variety of expressions that have been produced over decades, many even by our ancestors. Unlike the variety of blended whiskies that have been passed over, many of which have gone unrecorded, the single malts have pedigree attached to them. The age of the spirit, quantity of production, spirit strength and number of the bottle contribute to the value. The shape of bottle, colour of glass, method of manufacture, type of seal, label design and even packaging is important.

The purpose of this publication is a general reference for the collector and also the Scotch Whisky Industry since it is a central record of the majority of bottlings produced by The Industry spanning many decades.

I would like to thank my client base, both buyers and sellers, who have supported the auction evolution process over the years and the Scotch Whisky Industry for making the whole thing possible.

Martin Green
2007

Martin Green is Whisky Specialist at Bonhams
22 Queen Street
Edinburgh
EH2 1JX
0131 225 2266
01292 520000
martin.green@bonhams.com

Aberfeldy

The Aberfeldy Manager's Dram has proved to be very popular at auction, the limited edition bottling sold in 2002 and listed below is an example which was the first official release of the late 20th century and only given to those who attended a conference in 1987

Whisky Auction Sale Results (£s)	2000	2001	2002	2003	2004	2005	2006
Aberfeldy – 12-year-old (Signed by Distillery Manager)					20–24		
Aberfeldy – 13-year-old – 1978 (Signatory)	35						
Aberfeldy – 14-year-old – 1983 (Adelphi, 59.5%)							22
Aberfeldy – 15-year-old (Flora & Fauna)	38		40–45	20–48	40		38–75
Aberfeldy – 15-year-old (Pre-Flora & Fauna)					190		
Aberfeldy – 15-year-old (Limited edition of 1000, 1987)			360				
Aberfeldy – 16-year-old – 1966 (G & M)					80	80	
Aberfeldy – 15 year-old – 1969							90
Aberfeldy – 15-year-old – 1978 (Signatory)			55				
Aberfeldy – 16-year-old – 1969 (G & M)				100			
Aberfeldy – 16-year-old – 1970 (G & M)					80		
Aberfeldy – 17-year-old – 1969 (G & M)		100		80			
Aberfeldy – 19-year-old (Manager's Dram)	175–230	95–190	70–113	82–175	115–190	115–160	130–145
Aberfeldy – 25-year-old (Limited Release)		160		70	80–100	130	110
Aberfeldy – 26-year-old – 1975 (Cadenhead's, 57%)					45		
Aberfeldy – 1974 (G & M)		50	24		30-35	26	
Aberfeldy – 1975 (G & M, 40%)		30				45	
Aberfeldy – 1975 (SMWS, 56.4%)					33		
Aberfeldy – 1980 (62% vol)					32–50		55

Aberlour

Although the representation of Aberlour at auction is increasing, the results show that the earlier bottlings are most sought after and the presentation of the more contemporary bottlings is excellent

Whisky Auction Sale Results (£s)	2000	2001	2002	2003	2004	2005	2006
Aberlour – Glenlivet Centenary (crystal decanter)		260	170–190				
Aberlour – Glenlivet – 9-year-old (26 2/3 fl. oz, 70 proof)			60–110	115	45–85		80
Aberlour – Glenlivet – 12-year-old (75 cl., 40%)					70–85		
Aberlour – Glenlivet – 19-year-old – 1970 (Signatory, 46%)					32		
Aberlour – 5-year-old		125					
Aberlour Millennium – 10-year-old (12 bottles)	195–210				130	140–160	210
Aberlour VOHM – 10-year-old	70		50				
Aberlour – 10 year-old – Vintage 1979 (bottled for *The Times* newspaper)		70					
Aberlour – 10-year-old (70 cl., 40%, 6 bottles)			80				
Aberlour – 10-year-old (75 cl., 40%)				31			50
Aberlour – 10-year-old (3 boxed sets half bottles & glasses)					60		
Aberlour a'abundah Silver Label – 12-year-old (58.7%)			35–42	26	27	60	40–55
Aberlour – 12-year-old (75 cl., 40%)				30		50	
Aberlour – 15-year-old – 1988 (Old Malt Cask, 50%)					25		
Aberlour – 19-year-old – 1974 (First Cask)							25
Aberlour – 28-year-old – 1963 (Cadenhead's)			130				
Aberlour – 25-year-old – 1964	80–90	80–130	90	105	170	120	100–270

A *special Aberlour 1964*
signed by key personalities from
the year 1964 including
Harold Wilson, Julie Andrews,
Paul McCartney, George Harrison,
Ringo Starr and Ted Dexter.

Whisky Auction Sale Results (£s)	2000	2001	2002	2003	2004	2005	2006
Aberlour – 30-year-old – 1965			190	100			
Aberlour – 30-year-old – 1966							170
Aberlour – 22-year-old – 1969		140					
Aberlour – 22-year-old – 1976						50	90
Aberlour – Glenlivet Centenary – Over 21-year-old (Distilled 1958, ceramic jug)						420	
Aberlour – 21-year-old – 1970	90		80		110	70	100
Aberlour – 30-year-old – 1970						130	
Aberlour – 1970 (Bottled 1991, limited edition of 8000, 43%)					65		
Aberlour – 1985 (SMWS, 59.1%)		67					
Aberlour – 1985 (SMWS, 56.4%)							30

Ardbeg

The Spirit of Ardbeg is well represented at auction in a variety of ages and cask strengths, older bottlings fetch very healthy prices, the committee bottlings of older stock are proving to be very poprular too

Whisky Auction Sale Results (£s)	2000	2001	2002	2003	2004	2005	2006
Ardbeg – 1885 (A McDougall & Co)	1250						
Ardbeg – 1885 (A McDougall & Co, 15 U P)	3500						
Ardbeg – over 10-year-old – 1885 (A McDougall & Co, 15 U.P.)			1050				
Ardbeg – 10-year-old – Late 19th century	1450						
Ardbeg – 15-year-old – Late 19th century		2000					
Ardbeg – 9-year-old – Believed early 20th century		2000					

Left to right. Ardbeg Kildalton – 1980, Ardbeg – 17-year-old (Cadenhead's), Ardbeg – 1975, Ardbeg Lord of The Isles, Ardbeg – 1977

Whisky Auction Sale Results (£s)	2000	2001	2002	2003	2004	2005	2006
Ardbeg – 1904	2000						
Ardbeg (White Label)	190	160–190					
Ardbeg Committee Reserve (Bottled 2002, 55.3%)				180		110	
Ardbeg Very Young – 1997 (58.9%)						80	85
Ardbeg – 8-year-old – 1990 (Murray McDavid)	38						
Ardbeg – 8-year-old – 1991 (Murray McDavid)	38						
Ardbeg – 8-year-old – 1991 (Signatory, 43%)			88		37		
Ardbeg – 8-year-old – 1992 (non chill-filtered)			62				
Ardbeg – 8-year-old – 1992 (Signatory)	38			22			
Ardbeg – 9-year-old – 1991 (Signatory)	38						
Ardbeg – 10-year-old (26 2/3 fl. oz)	220–360		210–270		220		280–700

Whisky Auction Sale Results (£s)	2000	2001	2002	2003	2004	2005	2006
Ardbeg – 10-year-old (70 cl.)	110–160	160					
Ardbeg – 10-year-old (75 cl.)	60–155		155–210	195–200	180–270	220	290
Ardbeg – 10-year-old – 1990 (Old Malt Cask, 50%)		35	50				
Ardbeg – 10-year-old – 1991 (Cadenhead's, 60.3%)							40
Ardbeg – 12-year-old (26 2/3 fl. oz)	320		230				
Ardbeg – 12-year-old – 1967 (Cadenhead's, 80 degrees)							345
Ardbeg – 13-year-old – 1975 (Italian import, 54.8%)			140				
Ardbeg – 14-year-old – 1965 (Cadenhead's)			180				
Ardbeg – 14-year-old – 1972 (G & M, 40%)						290	
Ardbeg – 15-year-old (50 cl.)		105	80				
Ardbeg – 15-year-old – 1973 (Dun Eideann, 46%)		125					
Ardbeg – 16-year-old – 1961 (Cadenhead's, 46%)						280	
Ardbeg – 17-year-old – 1965 (G & M)				190			
Ardbeg – 17-year-old (Cadenhead's, 80 proof)	105	210					
Ardbeg – 17-year-old – 1976 (Cadenhead's, 49.8%)				300			
Ardbeg – 17-year-old (70 cl., 40%)	51			62		40	
Ardbeg – 18-year-old – 1974 (Cadenhead's, 57.6%)					135		
Ardbeg – 18-year-old – 1974 (W & M, 46%)		105					
Ardbeg – 18-year-old – 1975 (Signatory, 53.9%)			63				
Ardbeg – 19-year-old – 1974 (First Cask, 46%)				70			
Ardbeg – 19-year-old – 1974 (Signatory, 43%)	80		36–90				
Ardbeg – 19-year-old – 1974 (Italian Import, 40%)						120	
Ardbeg – 21-year-old – 1974 (Sestante, 40%)			90				
Ardbeg – 21-year-old (Committee, bottled 2001, 56.3%)				140–145	90–100	80–160	
Ardbeg – 21-year-old – 1974 (Bottled 2002, 44.5%)				340			

Whisky Auction Sale Results (£s)	2000	2001	2002	2003	2004	2005	2006
Ardbeg – 22-year-old – 1974 (Italian import)	135	100–140	125				
Ardbeg – 22-year-old – 1965 (Cadenhead's, 46%)					400		
Ardbeg – 23-year-old – 1974 (Signatory, 51.7%)	100						
Ardbeg – 23-year-old – 1974 (Signatory, 50.9%)							115
Ardbeg – 24-year-old – 1974 (Signatory, 51.3%)						95	
Ardbeg Lord of The Isles – 25-year-old (46%)					85	70–115	75–140
Ardbeg – 25-year-old (Milroy's, 58%)				70			
Ardbeg – 27-year-old – 1975 (Douglas Laing, 50%)					100	110	90
Ardbeg – 28-year-old – 1967 (Signatory, 53.2%)		130	88				
Ardbeg – 29-year-old – 1967 (Signatory, 52.8%)	170						
Ardbeg – 29-year-old – 1972 (Ardbeggeddon, 48.4%)				230–240			
Ardbeg – 29-year-old – 1972 (Douglas Laing, 50.4%)					120		
Ardbeg – 29-year-old – 1973 (Douglas Laing, 51.4%)						160–180	150
Ardbeg – 30-year-old (Wooden case, 70 cl.)		90–110	90–160	90–130	105–140	120–170	
Ardbeg – 30-year-old – 1963 (Sestante, 40%)	180	190–280					
Ardbeg – 30-year-old – 1967 (Signatory, 49.8%)	160				200		
Ardbeg – 30-year-old – 1967 (Signatory, 52%)		95	110		170		
Ardbeg – 30-year-old – 1967 (Signatory, 52.2%)			110				
Ardbeg – 30-year-old – 1973 (Douglas Laing, 51.9%)							150–180
Ardbeg – 30-year-old – 1975 (Douglas Laing, 47.8%)							170
Ardbeg – 32-year-old – 1966 (Cadenhead's, 42.8%)					210		
Ardbeg – 32-year-old – 1967 (Signatory, 47.5%)	105						
Ardbeg – 32-year-old – 1967 (Signatory, 43.1%)	105						
Ardbeg – 32-year-old – 1967 (Douglas Laing, 49%)				110			
Ardbeg – 1966 (SMWS, 50.5%)					270		

Whisky Auction Sale Results (£s)	2000	2001	2002	2003	2004	2005	2006
Ardbeg Single Cask – 1972 (48.3%)						150	270
Ardbeg – 1973 (G & M, 40%)						60–80	90
Ardbeg – 1974 (G & M, 40%)						70	90–100
Ardbeg – 1974 (G & M, 43%)						60	
Ardbeg Provenance – 1974 (55.6%)			240	200	170	200–260	290–380
Ardbeg – 1974 (Spirit of Scotland, 500 years)			90–110	80	80–140		
Ardbeg – 1974 (Botttled 1993, G & M)				90	33–66		
Ardbeg – 1974 (Bottled 1994, G & M)	35–46		65		80		
Ardbeg – 1974 (Bottled 1996, G & M)				70	85	60–80	
Ardbeg – 1974 (G & M, Spirit of Scotland, 40%)						120	
Ardbeg – 1974 (SMWS, 57.5%)		189					
Ardbeg – 1974 (Cask 2752, 52.1%)							220–240
Ardbeg – 1974 (Cask 3475, 44.5%)				160–180	240	200–260	
Ardbeg – 1975 (G & M, 40%)				75			45
Ardbeg – 1975 (43%)	30	60	43–65	75–110	95–125	45–100	90–140
Ardbeg – 1975 (Cask 4701, 46.2%)				120–140			
Ardbeg – 1975 (Cask 4718, 46.7%)	100						
Ardbeg – 1975 (Cask 4702, 45.2%)	100	230					
Ardbeg – 1976 (Cask 2391, 56%)	320–330					600	
Ardbeg – 1976 (Cask 2390, 53.1%)				180–210	260		
Ardbeg – 1976 (Cask 2392, 55%)				140–150	230–270	240	280
Ardbeg – 1976 (Cask 2394, 53.2%)				140–190	270		
Ardbeg – 1977 (46%)			35–40	30–45	60–105	65–70	55–95
Ardbeg – 1978 (43%)	23–30	60	35	60–85	70–95	55–70	100–145
Ardbeg – 1978 (G & M, 40%)			36	43		60	

Whisky Auction Sale Results (£s)	2000	2001	2002	2003	2004	2005	2006
Ardbeg – 1978 (Cadenhead's, 57.2%)	38						
Ardbeg – 1979 (G & M, 43%)							50
Ardbeg Kildalton – 1980 (57.6%)							160–260
Ardbeg – 1991 (Bottled 2001, Cadenhead's, 60.3%)					65		
Ardbeg Still Young – 1998 (56.2%)							55
Ardbeg Very Young – 1998 (58.3%)							55
Ardbeg Uigeadail – Bottled 2003 (54.2%)							38–55

Ardlussa

These are the only historical examples of bottles from Ardlussa Distillery to appear at auction over the last decade

Whisky Auction Sale Results (£s)	2000	2001	2002	2003	2004	2005	2006
Ardlussa – Distilled 1894 (J Ferguson & Sons)	1300–1900						

Ardmore

The very rare Ardmore – 15-year-old sold in 2001 fetched the highest price on record

Whisky Auction Sale Results (£s)	2000	2001	2002	2003	2004	2005	2006
Ardmore – 1977 (G & M)					25–32		
Ardmore – 1977 (Cadenhead's, Cask 7624, 60.5%)					52		
Ardmore – 1985 (G & M)			25				
Ardmore Centenary – 12-year-old – 1986	60–140			30–45	28–30	35	35–70
Ardmore – 13-year-old – 1978 (Cadenhead's, 61.1%)					25		
Ardmore Centenary – 21-year-old – 1977	310			200	70–120	150	160–180
Ardmore – 15-year-old (A hand bottling for Directors, 45.7%)		840		360	200		
Ardmore – 18-year-old – 1965 (Cadenhead's, 46%)			100		100	190	
Ardmore – 24-year-old – 1977 (Cadenhead's, 58.6%)							45

Ardmore – 15-year-old
(hand bottled)

Arran

The first release from Arran Distillery listed below shows a healthy auction result for such a young spirit

Whisky Auction Sale Results (£s)	2000	2001	2002	2003	2004	2005	2006
Isle of Arran (Robert Burns Federation)		40			50	47	27
Isle of Arran Founders' Reserve (43%)				40	30–50	27	20–25
Isle of Arran Scottish Painters' Collection No. 1					70		
Isle of Arran (Bottled 2002, 55.3%)							40
Isle of Arran (Bottled 2002, 56.2%)							30
Isle of Arran (Bottled 2003, 62.1%)							30
Isle of Arran (Bottled 2003, 57.4%)					35		
Isle of Arran (Bottled 2004, 59.4%)					60		
Isle of Arran – 3-year-old – 1995 (60.3%)		80–150	80	80–120			150
Isle of Arran – 7-year-old – 1995 (56.2%)			90				
Isle of Arran – 7-year-old (46%)						50	

Arran Founder's Reserve

Auchentoshan

The Auchentoshan QE II ship's crystal decanter is a fine example of this single malt

Whisky Auction Sale Results (£s)	2000	2001	2002	2003	2004	2005	2006
Auchentoshan (Eadie Cairns)	37		45–100			50–65	80
Auchentoshan Limited Edition, *Scottish Daily Record*					38		
Auchentoshan Lanark 850 – 10-year-old (stone jug)				70–90	95		80
Auchentoshan – 10-year-old (75 cl.)					62–65	33	
Auchentoshan – 12-year-old (75 cl.)		35		33			25
Auchentoshan Q E II – 12-year-old (75 cl., 43%)						45	
Auchentoshan – 12-year-old (Jet Stream, Prestwick, 70 cl.)			80				
Auchentoshan – 10-year-old (Jet Stream, Prestwick, 70 cl.)						180	60
Auchentoshan – 12-year-old (Eadie Cairns)			45–85		35		
Auchentoshan QE II Ship's Decanter – 12-year-old			130–140	280			
Auchentoshan – 12-year-old (Clydebank Centenary, stone jug)		45	40				
Auchentoshan – 15-year-old – 1981 (First Cask)		25			53	25	30
Auchentoshan – 18-year-old	33	20–45					
Auchentoshan – 18-year-old – 1978 (58.8%)							30
Auchentoshan – 20-year-old (Crystal decanter)			60				
Auchentoshan – 21-year-old (70 cl., 43%)						35	30–40
Auchentoshan – 20-year-old – 1984 (First Cask)					36		
Auchentoshan – 21-year-old – 1970 (43%)					35		
Auchentoshan – 21-year-old – 1974 (43%)				30			
Auchentoshan – 21-year-old – 1975 (55.4%)							50–65

Whisky Auction Sale Results (£s)	2000	2001	2002	2003	2004	2005	2006
Auchentoshan – 24-year-old – 1981 (Mission Series 5, 46%)							38
Auchentoshan – 29-year-old – 1973 (Archive, 55.8%)							80
Auchentoshan – 31-year-old – 1965 (Archive, 45.6%)					65	100	
Auchentoshan – 31-year-old – 1965 (Archive, 44.2%)							110
Auchentoshan – 31-year-old – 1965 (Archive, 45.2%)							130
Auchentoshan – 31-year-old – 1965 (Archive, 45.5%)							130
Auchentoshan – 31-year-old – 1966 (Archive, 46.1%)		60				100	
Auchentoshan – 31-year-old – 1966 (Archive, 47.6%)						110	140
Auchentoshan – Vintage 1966 (USA export, 86 proof)					65		
Auchentoshan – 1969 (BSD5750/ISO9002 Certificate)						360	
Auchentoshan – 1977 (SMWS, 55.5%)					55		

Auchentoshan (Eadie Carins)

Aultmore

Aultmore's appearance at auction shows that early distillery bottlings are highly popular and that the Centenary bottling stands out proudly over the others

Whisky Auction Sale Results (£s)	2000	2001	2002	2003	2004	2005	2006
Aultmore Centenary – 16-year-old (63%)	620–960	560–700		350		420–460	450–600
Aultmore – 7-year-old (Bottled 1997, Dun Eideann, 43%)				32			
Aultmore – 12-year-old (Harvey & Sons, 26 2/3 fl. oz)			75–180	100–190	105–160	140	160
Aultmore – 11-year-old – 1985 (Adelphi, 61.7%)				45			
Aultmore – 11-year-old – 1985 (Signatory, 43%)						30	
Aultmore – 12-year-old (Flora & Fauna)	38		26–36		29		38–75
Aultmore – 15-year-old – 1976 (Bristol Brandy Co, 43%)				46			
Autlmore – 15-year-old – 1985 (Adelphi, 60.1%)							22
Aultmore – 21-year-old – 1974 (Douglas Laing, 60.9%)						30	
Aultmore – 21-year-old – 1974 (60.9%)							180
Aultmore – 1973 (Italian import, 46%)			120				
Aultmore – 1983 (58.8%)	40				20	35–40	52–85
Aultmore – 10-year-old – 1990 (Hart Bros)		30					

Left to right.
Aultmore Centenary,
Aultmore – 12-year-old

Balblair

The few expressions of Balblair that have been seen at auction so far include a small range of bottlings by Gordon & MacPhail, the recent distillery bottling fetching the most

Whisky Auction Sale Results (£s)	2000	2001	2002	2003	2004	2005	2006
Balblair (G & M, 100 proof)			90				
Balblair V H Small Still (G & M, 26 2/3 fl. oz)			90				
Balblair – 5-year-old (75 cl.)		50–60		72			
Balblair – 8-year-old (G & M, 26 2/3 fl. oz)					53		
Balblair – 10-year-old (G & M)			21		23–52		
Balblair – 12-year-old – 1965 (Cadenhead's, 45.7%)			55		80		
Balblair – 15-year-old – 1964 (G & M)	200			90		120	
Balblair – 18-year-old – 1964 (G & M)						120	
Balblair – 20-year-old – 1964 (G & M)				80			
Balblair – 22-year-old – 1975 (First Cask)					28	20	
Balblair – 31-year-old – 1969 (45%)							45
Balblair – 33-year-old (45.4%)		90			130	90	100–130
Balblair – 33-year-old – 1965 (Douglas Laing, 44%)						80	
Balblair – 34-year-old – 1965 (Douglas Laing, 40.1%)							80
Balblair – 37-year-old – 1965 (Adelphi, 54.3%)							50
Balblair – 1989 (46%)					29		

Balmenach

The expressions of Balmenach that have been seen at auction to date include distillery bottlings and others by independent bottlers

Whisky Auction Sale Results (£s)	2000	2001	2002	2003	2004	2005	2006
Balmenach Whisky – 1910 (12 under proof)				210			
Balmenach – 10-year-old (Scottish Wildlife)			42				27
Balmenach – 12-year-old (Flora & Fauna)	38	30		30–35	26		37–75
Balmenach – 12-year-old – 1970 (G & M)						100	
Balmenach – 15-year-old – 1982 (Adelphi, 63.4%)						32	22
Balmenach – 16-year-old – 1968 (G & M)							85
Balmenach – 16-year-old – 1970 (G & M)				60	75		
Balmenach – 16-year-old – 1970 (G & M, low level)							36
Balmenach – 18-year-old – 1979 (Hart Bros)					31	20	35
Balmenach – Glenlivet – 19-year-old – 1961 (Cadenhead's, 46%)					105–110		
Balmenach-Glenlivet – 21-year-old – 1961 (Cadenhead's, 46%)							110
Balmenach – Glenlivet – 24-year-old – 1961 (Cadenhead's, 46%)					110	85	
Balmenach – 25-year-old – 1972 (Hart Bros)					31		35
Balmenach – 25-year-old (Queen's Golden Jubilee, 58%)				100		85	110
Balmenach – 28-year-old – 1966 (Whisky Connoisseur, 63.5%)	75						
Balmenach – 1970 (G & M)					33		
Balmenach – 27-year-old – 1973 (46%)					60		30
Balmenach – 28-year-old – 1972 (46%)					100		45

Whisky Auction Sale Results (£s)	2000	2001	2002	2003	2004	2005	2006
Balmenach – Glenlivet – 30-year-old – 1971 (Cadenhead's, 49.3%)					70		
Balmenach – 30-year-old – 1972 (Hart Bros)			32			40	
Balmenach – 1971 (G & M)			24			38	
Balmenach – 1972 (G & M)					35		
Balmenach – 1973 (G & M)	22		22		22	38	
Balmenach – 1978 (SMWS, 48.3%)							70
Balmenach – 1987 (G & M)							37

Balmenach-Glenlivet – 24-year-old
(Cadenhead's)

Balvenie

Old and rare survivors of Balvenie perform very well at auction, the 50-year-old bottled in the 1980's is very popular when it makes an appearance and the variety of Vintage Cask Selections can be difficult to find

Whisky Auction Sale Results (£s)	2000	2001	2002	2003	2004	2005	2006
Balvenie – Glenlivet 'As We Get It'	160				55		75
Balvenie Founders Reserve (Cognac shaped)		60–85	31–65	50–90	50–80	55–80	75–110
Balvenie Founders Reserve (Cognac shaped, for Pauls & Sanders)							240
Balvenie – Glenlivet – Over-8-year-old	160					180–200	
Balvenie Over Proof – 8-year-old (26 2/3 fl. ozs)			31–86	97–170	100–160		
Balvenie – 15-year-old (Sandy Grant Gordon Celebration Bottling, 50.4%)		90	120			90	60
Balvenie Classic (75 cl.)					50		130–210
Balvenie Classic – 18-year-old		85			55		
Balvenie – 50-year-old – 1937	1100–1700	1600					2500
Balvenie Over Proof – 1952 (Robert Watson, 1.5 over proof)					350		
Balvenie Over Proof – 1953 (Robert Watson, 1.5 over proof)					280	170	
Balvenie Vintage Cask – 1961 (49.3%)			330				
Balvenie Over Proof – 1965 (R. Watson, Aberdeen)			55		200		
Balvenie Vintage Cask – 1966 (42.6%)					140		240
Balvenie Vintage Cask – 1966 (44.6%)						145	
Balvenie Vintage Cask – 1967 (49.7%)			180–200	180	200		
Balvenie Vintage Cask – 1968 (50.8%)					185		
Balvenie – Glenlivet – 12-year-old – 1979 (Cadenhead's, 59.5%)						80	
Balvenie – 15-year-old – Vintage 1974 (Prestonfield House)			100				

THE BALVENIE®

By marrying The Balvenie slowly aged in traditional oak casks with that aged in oloroso sherry butts, the Balvenie Malt Master, David Stewart, has created a rich, mellow whisky with unusual depth and complexity. The traditional oak - previously used to mature Bourbon - imbues warm honeyed tones, intense floral sweetness and distinct notes of vanilla, whereas The Balvenie matured in sherry wood displays a rich depth of colour, a dry oakiness and even greater refinement.

To create The Balvenie Portwood 21 Year Old, rare 21 Year Old Balvenie - which has been matured in traditional oak casks - is transferred to a port cask, or pipe, which has held fine port wines. Here it is sampled every month by David Stewart to ensure that just the right amount of character is imparted by the port casks, enhancing and developing the single malt, whilst preserving its original characteristics.

Whisky Auction Sale Results (£s)	2000	2001	2002	2003	2004	2005	2006
Balvenie – 15-year-old – 1974 (Signatory, 43%)		80			45	30–50	
Balvenie – 1975 (57.1%)				35			
Balvenie Single Barrel – 15-year-old – 1977 (50.4%)		60		50		42	75
Balvenie Single Barrel – 15-year-old – 1978 (50.4%)				30			
Balvenie Single Barrel – 15-year-old – 1979 (50.4%)					30		
Balvenie Single Barrel – 15-year-old – 1980 (50.4%)		30					
Balvenie Classic – 18-year-old		80	45			87	
Balvenie – 20-year-old – 1972 (First Cask)						165	110
Balvenie Double Wood – 21-year-old					65		
Balvenie Port Wood – 21-year-old							40
Balvenie Single Barrel – 25-year-old – 1974 (46.9%)							110–120

Left to right. The Balvenie Classic – 18-year-old, The Balvenie Over Proof (Robert Watson), The Balvenie – Over 8-year-old

COLLECTING MALT WHISKY – A PRICE GUIDE

Banff

The variety of expressions of Banff that have been seen at auction so far are all independent bottlings, the majority at cask strength

Whisky Auction Sale Results (£s)	2000	2001	2002	2003	2004	2005	2006
Banff – 13-year-old – 1974 (G & M)					80	80–95	
Banff – 15-year-old – 1964 (Cadenhead's, 45.7%)	110		60			77	130–160
Banff – 1974 (G & M)	22		27–60	20	25–40	25	60
Banff – 1977 (SMWS, 61.7%)							95
Banff – 1978 (Captain Burns)					35		
Banff – 1975 (G & M, Spirit of Scotland)					37		
Banff – 15-year-old – 1976 (Cadenhead's, 61.1%)					43		
Banff – 18-year-old – 1978 (Silent Stills)			65				
Banff – 18-year-old – 1980 (Ian MacLeod, 43%)				25			
Banff – 18-year-old – 1981 (Old Malt Cask, 50%)	22						
Banff – 20-year-old – 1976 (Cadenhead's, 56.4%)			40	30			
Banff – 21-year-old – 1976 (Cadenhead's, 58.2%)			40	30			
Banff – 23-year-old – 1976 (Signatory, 55.5%)					36		
Banff – 23-year-old – 1979 (Ian MacLeod, 46%)							60
Banff – 31-year-old – 1966 (Old Malt Cask, 50%)	30–60		65				60
Banff – 34-year-old – 1966 (Old Malt Cask, 45.8%)		100–110					
Banff – 36-year-old – 1966 (Old Malt Cask, 42.1%)					90		60

Ben Nevis

The variety of expressions of Ben Nevis that have appeared at auction recently are all cask strength examples

Whisky Auction Sale Results (£s)	2000	2001	2002	2003	2004	2005	2006
Ben Nevis – 10-year-old – 1992 (55.2%)							48
Ben Nevis – 14-year-old – 1965 (Cadenhead's, 46%)	95						120
Ben Nevis – 15-year-old – 1977 (Cadenhead's, 46%)							30
Ben Nevis – 16-year-old – 1965 (Cadenhead's, 46%)					57		
Ben Nevis – 19-year-old – 1976 (60.4%)					55		
Ben Nevis – 21-year-old – 1972 (55.6%)				110			
Ben Nevis – 22-year-old – 1965 (Cadenhead's, 46%)						90–110	
Ben Nevis – 24-year-old – 1965 (Cadenhead's, 46%)			45				
Ben Nevis – 25-year-old – 1966 (Crystal decanter, 59%)				210			
Ben Nevis – 26-year-old – 1966 (59%)	145						
Ben Nevis – 26-year-old – 1967 (58%)				100			
Ben Nevis – 26-year-old – 1969 (54%)				150			
Ben Nevis – 26-year-old – 1968 (54.6%)			90				
Ben Nevis – 26-year-old – 1970 (52%)						80	
Ben Nevis – 26-year-old – 1971 (53.6%)						85	
Ben Nevis – 26-year-old – 1974 (53.4%)					70		
Ben Nevis – 26-year-old – 1975 (53.8%)						65	
Ben Nevis – 30-year-old – 1971 (56.9%)							130
Ben Nevis – 33-year-old – 1963 (Signatory, 54.2%)						65	
Ben Nevis – 1966 (SMWS, 55%)						100	
Ben Nevis – 35-year-old – 1967 (Hart Bros, 50.1%)			33			60	

Whisky Auction Sale Results (£s)	2000	2001	2002	2003	2004	2005	2006
Ben Nevis – 1970 (Italian import, 46%)			122				
Ben Nevis – 1977 (SMWS, 62.1%)					55		
Ben Nevis – 1977 (Cadenhead's, 60.9%)					52		

Ben Nevis – 14-year-old
(Cadenhead's)

Ben Wyvis

Some of the very finest expressions of Ben Wyvis have appeared at auction, they have commanded much interest and respectable prices

Whisky Auction Sale Results (£s)	2000	2001	2002	2003	2004	2005	2006
Ben Wyvis (Robert Dunbar & Co)	1300						
Ben Wyvis – Over 12-year-old – Bottled 1894 (Half bottle)		1100					
Ben Wyvis – Over 12-year-old – Bottled 1894	3000						
Ben Wyvis – 10-year-old (Canadian Export, 43%)						550	
Ben Wyvis – 32-year-old – 1968 (Signatory)	580	600					
Ben Wyvis – 27-year-old – 1972 (43.1%)		600–620		170			
Ben Wyvis – 27-year-old – 1972 (45.9%)				150		460	
Ben Wyvis – 27-year-old – 1972 (Invergordon, 43%)				460	420		
Ben Wyvis – 27-year-old – 1972 (Ben Wyvis Distillery, 43%)				420		410	290–350
Ben Wyvis – 37-year-old – 1965 (Signed by Richard Paterson, 44%)					560–600	560	
Ben Wyvis – 1972 (Bottled for Munton & Fison, 54.4%)					800		
Ben Wyvis Laboratory sample – 1973	320						

Ben Wyvis – 37-year-old

Benachie

These are the only historical examples of bottles from Benachie Distillery to appear at auction over the last decade

Whisky Auction Sale Results (£s)	2000	2001	2002	2003	2004	2005	2006
Benachie – 1895 (Calander & Graham)		3200					
Benachie – 1895 (Calander & Graham, half bottle)		1600					

Benachie – 1895

Benmore

This is the only historical example of a bottle from Benmore Distillery to sell at auction over the last decade

Whisky Auction Sale Results (£s)	2000	2001	2002	2003	2004	2005	2006
Benmore – 1896 (Bulloch Lade & Co)	1900						

Benriach

A small selection of expressions of Benriach have been seen at auction recently

Whisky Auction Sale Results (£s)	2000	2001	2002	2003	2004	2005	2006
Benriach – 10-year-old – 1969 (G & M)		100	70	90			
Benriach – 12-year-old – 1986 (Adelphi, 60.3%)							20
Benriach – 12-year-old – 1969 (G & M)						95	
Benriach-Glenlivet – 13-year-old – 1966 (Cadenhead's)							115
Benriach – 34-year-old – 1968 (Hart Bros, 49.8%)					50		42
Benriach – 1969 (G & M)			60		50		
Benriach – 1976 (G & M)					31–42		
Benriach – 1980 (G & M, 59.3%)	43						
Benriach – 1982 (G & M)		38		25	33		32
Benriach – 1982 (G & M, 62.9%)					33–46		
Benriach – 1982 (SMWS, 62.6%)					100		

Benriach-Glenlivet
(Cadenhead's)

Benrinnes

The Benrinnes Manager's Drams show a very healthy growth and are very sought after when they appear at auction

Whisky Auction Sale Results (£s)	2000	2001	2002	2003	2004	2005	2006
Benrinnes – 11-year-old – 1968 (G & M)			70	110			
Benrinnes – 12-year-old (Manager's Dram)	153–193		90–220	130–210	130–170		180
Benrinnes – 12-year-old (MacArthur, 63.6%)			37				
Benrinnes – 12-year-old – 1968 (G & M)					80	70	
Benrinnes – 14-year-old – 1979 (Adelphi, 65.6%)							22
Benrinnes – 18-year-old – 1962 (Cadenhead's, 46%)							200
Benrinnes – 15-year-old (Flora & Fauna)	38		20–35	31	15–40		35–37
Benrinnes – 17-year-old – 1968 (G & M)					55		
Benrinnes – 17-year-old – 1980 (Hart Bros)		27				25	
Benrinnes Centenary Reserve –1978 (G & M)					50		
Benrinnes – 18-year-old – 1979 (Hart Bros)					25	20–40	
Benrinnes – 19-year-old (Crystal decanter, Italian import, 57.1%)	420						
Benrinnes – 1972 (G & M)						38	
Benrinnes – 21-year-old – 1974 (Douglas Laing, 60.4%)	36–46	37			27	30	45
Benrinnes – 1974 (SMWS, 56.4%)						60–75	
Benrinnes – 36-year-old – 1963 (Cadenhead's, 51.9%)			170		90–100		

Benromach

A small slection of expressions of Benromach have been seen at auction in recent years

Whisky Auction Sale Results (£s)	2000	2001	2002	2003	2004	2005	2006
Benromach – 12-year-old					40		
Benromach – 15-year-old			32–40				
Benromach Centenary – 17-year-old			32–40	75	40–48	80	60
Benromach – 18-year-old					32		
Benromach – 14-year-old – 1965 (Cadenhead's)			45		110		
Benromach – 14-year-old – 1968 (G & M)						80–90	
Benromach – 16-year-old – 1968 (G & M)							88
Benromach – 18-year-old – 1976 (Hart Bros)				63			
Benromach – 19-year-old (45%)						20	
Benromach – 25-year-old (43%)						20–25	
Benromach – 27-year-old – 1968 (Hart Bros)	43	33				27	
Benromach – 1969 (G & M)	43				50		
Benromach – 1970 (G & M)					27–40		
Benromach – 1971 (G & M)			32–36		42	37	33
Benromach – 1972 (G & M)						25	
Benromach – Vintage 1973 (G & M)						22	60
Benromach – Vintage 1974 (G & M)					40–60	22	

Bladnoch

The selection of expressions of Bladnoch that have been seen at auction so far show that older bottlings fetch the best prices

Whisky Auction Sale Results (£s)	2000	2001	2002	2003	2004	2005	2006
Bladnoch Believed – 1842 (Un-labelled)					150		
Bladnoch (75 cl.)	85	100	80–90		105–130		
Bladnoch – 8-year-old (Arthur Bell, 75 cl.)	70		35		65–90	90–100	
Bladnoch – 10-year-old (James MacArthur)					20		
Bladnoch – 11-year-old – 1988 (Signatory, 43%)							20
Bladnoch – 12-year-old (Flora & Fauna)	38		32–33	36		38–48	25–75
Bladnoch – 12-year-old – 1987 (Signatory)			20				
Bladnoch – 13-year-old – 1964 (Cadenhead's)		120				125	115
Bladnoch – 15-year-old – 1967 (G & M)							85
Bladnoch – 15-year-old – 1980 (Cadenhead's, 58%)							30
Bladnoch – 16-year-old – 1980 (First Cask)			50		32–36	25	
Bladnoch – 19-year-old – 1980 (Silent Stills)	52						
Bladnoch – 22-year-old – 1974 (Adelphi, 54.3%)							60
Bladnoch – 23-year-old – 1966 (Signatory, 43%)						70	
Bladnoch – 23-year-old – 1977 (53.6%)							85
Bladnoch – 26-year-old – 1974 (Signatory)				25–60			
Bladnoch – 34-year-old – 1958 (Cadenhead's)					130		
Bladnoch – 1974 (G & M)				27			
Bladnoch – 1984 (G & M)		26					
Bladnoch – 1986 (G & M)						25	
Bladnoch – 1990 (Glenborrodale Castle, 46%)					38		

Blair Athol

Limited edition and celebration bottlings of Blair Athol attract the most interest and fetch the higher prices at auction

Whisky Auction Sale Results (£s)	2000	2001	2002	2003	2004	2005	2006
Blair Athol – 8-year-old (Arthur Bell & Sons)		70–95	25–60	40–130	40–65		200
Blair Athol – 8-year-old (Athol Distilleries)		120					
Blair Athol – 10-year-old (Dunfermline Society, Millennium, 43%)		50					
Blair Athol – 10-year-old (Dunfermline Society, Millennium, 59.7%)		80–90					
Blair Athol Bicentenary – 12-year-old		700		480			
Blair Athol – 12-year-old (Athol Distilleries)	75			135			

Left to right.
Blair Athol – 12-year-old
(Athol Distilleries),
Blair Athol Bicentenary
– 18-year-old,
Blair Athol – 8-year-old
(Arthur Bell & Sons)

Whisky Auction Sale Results (£s)	2000	2001	2002	2003	2004	2005	2006
Blair Athol – 12-year-old (Flora & Fauna)	38	20		26	23–26		20–38
Blair Athol – 12-year-old – 1956 (Cadenhead's, 45.7%)						65	
Blair Athol – 15-year-old (Manager's Dram)	60–180	70–183	40–127	60–100	55–95	85–100	85–105
Blair Athol Bicentenary – 18-year-old (56.7%)	50–150	45–90	42–65	40–55	45–70	48	70–75
Blair Athol – 20-year-old – 1977 (Signatory, 43%)							20
Blair Athol – 21-year-old – 1973 (First Cask)					32–34	40	
Blair Athol – 21-year-old – 1974 (First Cask)			33				
Blair Athol – 26-year-old – 1976 (First Cask)					40–52		
Blair Athol – 27-year-old – 1975 (54.7%)							50
Blair Athol – 1966 (Cadenhead's, 57.1%)			140				
Blair Athol – 1981 (55.5%)			24		35		

Bowmore

The Black Bowmore is a jewel in Bowmore's crown, the Mutter bottle caused a great sensation when it fetched a then world record price in 2001 and The Queen's Cask bottled in 2003 to celebrate Her Majesty's Golden Jubilee raised a remarkable £8000 for charity

Whisky Auction Sale Results (£s)	2000	2001	2002	2003	2004	2005	2006
Bowmore – Late 19th century (Mutter bottle)		13,000					
Bowmore Blair Castle Horse Trials – 2000		2100	650		750	500	580
Bowmore Blair Castle Horse Trials – 2001			650		620	520	
Bowmore Blair Castle Horse Trials – 2002					750		
Bowmore Blair Castle Horse Trials – 2003						480–560	580
Bowmore Blair Castle Horse Trials – 2004					620	420–500	580
Bowmore Fly Fishing Championships – 2003					780	350–480	490

Left to right.
Bowmore – Late 19th-Century
(Mutter bottle), Bowmore
Blair Castle Horse Trials,
Bowmore (Sherriff's)

Bowmore is one of the most collectable and celebrated single malts that appear at auction. Among the most popular bottlings is the Bicentenary released in 1979 that now sells for over £450 per bottle at auction. The bottle design was taken from an example held in the Morrison family archives which is believed to date to the 18th Century.

Pictured below are vintages of Bowmore released in the 1980's, the 1956 example now fetches as much as £450 per bottle. Black Bowmore first relased in 1993 then conscutively until 1995 when the final release was launched, first made an appearance at auction in 1997 when it fetched £250, nine years later this fine and rare bottling now realises as much as £1600 per bottle, this fact illustrates what a good investment single malt whisky can be in the long term.

In 2003 the world record for a 21-year-old malt was broken, a 21-year-old Bowmore distilled in

1980 was sold at auction for an incredible £8000, the bottling was The Queen's Cask given to Her Majesty The Queen on her visit to the distillery on Islay and bottled in the year of Her Majesty's Golden Jubilee, the sale proceeds were donated to charity.

In 2004 another record for the sale of a 15-year-old single malt was made, Bowmore Beach Rugby Tournament was sold at a charity auction on Islay for £3800, another fantastic price for such a young spirit, the sale

proceeds were also given to charity.

Other fine examples of Bowmore are the 1955 stoneware jug bottled to commemorate the opening of the reception centre at the distillery in 1974, only 13 fluid ounces in size that fetches up to £500 and 12-year-old malt distilled in 1965 independently bottled that fetches £250 at auction, in fact any rare examples of Bowmore are highly sought after by collectors.

Whisky Auction Sale Results (£s)	2000	2001	2002	2003	2004	2005	2006
Bowmore Claret Wood Finish	60–90	80–100	40–110	27–60	45–57	25–50	40–45
Bowmore Cask Strength (56%)							40
Bowmore Darkest			55	20–27		32	24–25
Bowmore Dawn						32	24
Bowmore Dusk (Claret Casked)		25	35	20–27		32	24
Bowmore Golf Decanter (No age statement)					120		
Bowmore QE II (Stone jug)					60–70		
Bowmore Voyage (Port Casked, 56%)		25	30–35	23–27	45–57	35–50	24
Bowmore (Sherriff's)	150–340	230	220		300–380		
Bowmore (Morrison's, brown, dumpy)			86–150	150	160		150
Bowmore De Luxe (James Kilpatrick & Son, brown, dumpy)			85–145				
Bowmore Cask Strength (56%)				70		33	
Bowmore – 7-year-old (Sherriff's)	80–280	160–220	200				
Bowmore – 8-year-old (Sherriff's)	260		180–360			350	
Bowmore Triple – 8-year-old	110						
Bowmore Vatted Malt – 8-year-old (IWSC, 1995)				90–110	150	55–130	100
Bowmore – 10-year-old (Prestonfield House)			65				
Bowmore – 10-year-old (Forth Road Bridge, jug)			140	100		160	70–90
Bowmore – 10-year-old (Stone jug, limited edition 400)					100	80	50
Bowmore – 10-year-old (Glasgow Garden Festival, 1988)					150–160	50–80	70–95
Bowmore – 11-year-old – 1979 (Cadenhead's, 58.4%)					150		
Bowmore – 12-year-old – 1965 (Cadenhead's)	220		170				250
Bowmore – 12-year-old – 1983 (Cadenhead's, 60.4%)			36	45			
Bowmore – 12-year-old (Morrison's, brown, dumpy)			43–100	47–70	87–130	92–140	60–135

Whisky Auction Sale Results (£s)	2000	2001	2002	2003	2004	2005	2006
Bowmore – Over-12-year-old (Morrison Howat, 54.5%)							195
Bowmore – 13-year-old – 1965 (Cadenhead's, 45.7%)							210
Bowmore – 13-year-old – 1966 (Cadenhead's, 45.7%)						300	
Bowmore – 13-year-old – 1988 (Provenance, 43%)							25
Bowmore – 12-year-old (Provident Mutual)		200					
Bowmore – 14-year-old (Italian Import, 40%)						70	
Bowmore – 15-year-old (Glasgow Garden Festival, jug)		70	61–67	73	75	100	65
Bowmore – 15-year-old – 1971 (59.1%)							150
Bowmore – 18-year-old – 1971 (40%)							150
Bowmore – 20-year-old – 1973 (56.8%)	80						
Bowmore – 20-year-old – 1965 (Italian Import, 43%)							190
Bowmore – 20-year-old – 1983 (Douglas Laing, 50%)							50
Bowmore – 21-year-old (43%)					60		55–90
Bowmore Blended – 21-year-old						60–140	70
Bowmore – 21-year-old – 1970 (43%)						120	
Bowmore – 21-year-old – 1971 (43%)					120		
Bowmore – 21-year-old – 1973 (43%)			170		85	100	
Bowmore Queen's Cask – 21-year-old – 1980 (51.1%)				8000			
Bowmore – 21-year-old Golf decanter	125	130–190	210				380
Bowmore – 21-year-old Crystal decanter		190					
Bowmore – 22-year-old Ceramic bottle	80		75	70–80	60–90	110	90
Bowmore – 22-year-old – Vintage 1965 (Prestonfield House)			400				460–580
Bowmore – 22-year-old – 1982 (First Cask)							50
Bowmore – 24-year-old – 1974 (First Cask)		73–83					70

YOU'VE PERFECTED
YOUR TASTE IN ART.

YOUR TASTE IN MUSIC.

NOW PERFECT IT
IN SINGLE MALTS.

THE ORIGINAL ISLAY SINGLE MALT WHISKY.

Whisky Auction Sale Results (£s)	2000	2001	2002	2003	2004	2005	2006
Bowmore – 25-year-old Ceramic bottle					90–130	80–110	90–145
Bowmore – 25-year-old (43%)						80–90	90
Bowmore Auld Alliance Chateau La Grange – 25-year-old				880		680–1100	
Bowmore – 25-year-old – 1973 (Kingsbury & Co, 46%)		100	85				105
Bowmore – 25-year-old – 1963 (Hart Bros, 43%)		100					
Bowmore – 25-year-old – 1965 (Hart Bros, 43%)		100					
Bowmore – 25-year-old – 1968 (43%)			290				170
Bowmore – 25-year-old – 1969		90			70		
Bowmore Blended – 27-year-old	230–260	260–290	160	160		90	95–170
Bowmore – 27-year-old – 1972		380	130–270	160		160	130–160
Bowmore – 27-year-old – 1973 (Blackadder, 50.2%)							130

Left to right.
Bowmore – 1955, Bowmore – 1956,
Bowmore – 1963, Bowmore – 1964,
Bowmore – 12-year-old (Cadenhead's)

Opposite page, left to right.
Bowmore – 32-year-old – 1968,
Bowmore – 27-year-old – 1972,
Bowmore – 21-year-old – 1980 –
The Queen's Cask

Whisky Auction Sale Results (£s)	2000	2001	2002	2003	2004	2005	2006
Bowmore – 30-year-old (Ceramic bottle)	100		105	100	120–160	60–130	120
Bowmore – 30-year-old Anniversary – 1963		500–520	480–500		380–470	400–620	
Bowmore Islay Legend – 30-year-old – 1963						1300	
Bowmore – 30-year-old – 1972 (Signatory, 49.7%)						50	100
Bowmore Dynasty Decanter – 31-year-old (Hart Bros)				520			
Bowmore – 31-year-old – 1968 (Signatory, 43%)		55					
Bowmore – 31-year-old – 1969 (Old Malt Cask)			130				
Bowmore – 32-year-old – 1968 (45.5%)			180–240	150–220	140–190	160–190	190–260
Bowmore – 32-year-old – 1968 (Signatory, 46.2%)		100					100
Bowmore – 34-year-old – 1966 (Hart Bros, 42.6%)							180
Bowmore – 35-year-old – 1968 (Celtic Heartlands, 40.6%)						147	173

Whisky Auction Sale Results (£s)	2000	2001	2002	2003	2004	2005	2006
Bowmore – 35-year-old – 1964 (42.1%, 99 bottles)		1900–2100	1300	1300–1500			2200
Bowmore – 35-year-old – 1966 (Hart Bros, 43.7%)		95					105
Bowmore – 36-year-old – 1966 (Peerless Collection, 45.3%)					90		
Bowmore – 38-year-old – 1957 (40.1%, 861 bottles)					800	550–620	750
Bowmore Oloroso Cask – 38-year-old – 1964 (42.9%, 300 bottles)					850	850	
Bowmore Bourbon Cask – 38-year-old – 1964 (43.2%, 300 bottles)					800	850	
Bowmore Fino Cask – 37 year-old – 1964 (49.6%, 300 bottles)				1100		850–1000	1050
Bowmore Bicentenary	120–260	270–300	250–320	290–370	250–420	290–450	330–490
Bowmore Bicentenary (Lacking box)			210			200	300–440
Bowmore Bicentenary (Italian import)		280					
Bowmore – 1955 (13 fl. ozs, stone jug)	510	480	270				420–510
Bowmore – 1956	460		420	440	320–360	350	450
Bowmore – 1957 (Moon import)	250						
Bowmore – 1962 (Moon import)	200	440					
Bowmore – 1963			260		250		420
Bowmore – 1964			400				390
Bowmore (Black) – 1964	680–1500	750–1350	790–1160	850–1100	850–1350	800–1500	950–1600
Bowmore – 1965 (50%)		400	170–210			390	
Bowmore – 1966		260					
Bowmore – 1967	165	230	240				
Bowmore – 1969	85		190				

Whisky Auction Sale Results (£s)	2000	2001	2002	2003	2004	2005	2006
Bowmore – 1972 (SMWS 5th Anniversary)						230	
Bowmore – 1973	85				190–220	255–460	
Bowmore – 1976 (55.3%)						160	
Bowmore – 1976 (SMWS)							130
Bowmore – 1979 (Cadenhead's)			200				
Bowmore – 1984 (58.8%)				25–38	60–75	50	40
Bowmore – 1989 (51.8%)							30
Bowmore – 1990 (53.8%)							40

Left to right. Bowmore – 22-year-old, Bowmore – 30-year-old, Bowmore – 25-year-old, Bowmore Bi-centenary

Brora

The Brora cask strength Rare Malts have been popular when they appear at auction

Whisky Auction Sale Results (£s)	2000	2001	2002	2003	2004	2005	2006
Brora – 13-year-old – 1982 (Cadenhead's, 60.4%)					50		
Brora – 18-year-old – 1981 (Signatory, 46%)			62	25–37			
Brora – 18-year-old – 1981 (Douglas Laing, 50%)					35		
Brora – 19-year-old – 1981 (Prestonfield House, 58.8%)					75		
Brora – 21-year-old – 1977 (56.9%)			42–57		55	45	65
Brora – 21-year-old – 1982 (Old Malt Cask, 50%)						30	
Brora – 24-year-old – 1977 (56.1%)					52–55	45	62–65
Brora – 20-year-old – 1975 (59.1%)						45–90	72–105
Brora – 20-year-old – 1975 (60.75%)	27						
Brora – 20-year-old – 1975 (54.9%)			46	27–40		60	55
Brora – 20-year-old – 1982 (Ian MacLeod, 46%)						55	
Brora – 22-year-old – 1972 (58.7%)	155–260	58	80		56–83	107	
Brora – 22-year-old – 1972 (60.2%)					180		
Brora – 22-year-old – 1972 (61.1%)					76	175	
Brora – 1972 (G & M)		50	25	26–46	33–85	40–77	
Brora – 1981 (Lombard, 50%)					35		
Brora – 1982 (G & M)					35		
Brora – 28-year-old – 1971 (Old Malt Cask, 50%)							110
Brora – 29-year-old – 1971 (Old Malt Cask, 50%)	90						110
Brora – 29-year-old – 1972 (Old Malt Cask, 51%)					110	100	
Brora – 30-year-old (55.7%)						105–110	

Whisky Auction Sale Results (£s)	2000	2001	2002	2003	2004	2005	2006
Brora – 30-year-old – 1972 (Old Malt Cask, 49.7%)					90–95	80	150
Brorageddon – 30-year-old – 1972 (Old Malt Cask, 50.8%)					210		
Brora – 32-year-old – 1970 (Old Malt Cask, 58.4%)					90	95–105	100

Brora – 28-year-old – 1971
(Douglas Laing)

Bruichladdich

Many cask strength examples of this very fine Islay malt have appeared at auction with healthy prices being achieved

Whisky Auction Sale Results (£s)	2000	2001	2002	2003	2004	2005	2006
Bruichladdich (75 degrees, 26 2/3 fl. oz)			96		130		70
Bruichladdich Centenary Glass Decanter							140–180
Bruichladdich XVII							25–37
Bruichladdich – 10-year-old (75 cl.)		65	25	47	25–65	50–72	50–110
Bruichladdich – 10-year-old – 1965 (Italian import)	90						
Bruichladdich – 10-year-old (ceramic decanter)					30		
Bruichladdich – 13-year-old – 1989 (57.1%)							47
Bruichladdich Links – 14-year-old (46%)							45–47
Bruichladdich – 15-year-old (ceramic decanter)	95	50			42–50		50
Bruichladdich – 15-year-old (75 cl.)			21–23		43		40–42
Bruichladdich – 15-year-old – 1986 (Cask 356, 46%)							85
Bruichladdich – 17-year-old		60					
Bruichladdich Enlightenment – 18-year-old – 1984 (53.7%)					180	115–120	120–130
Bruichladdich – 20-year-old 1st edition						50	40–55
Bruichladdich Flirtation – 20-year-old 2nd edition (46%)					80		35
Bruichladdich – 20-year-old – 1969 (Signatory, 43%)	60	60	40		45		
Bruichladdich – 20-year-old (46%, 70 cl.)				35		50–55	25
Bruichladdich – 21-year-old		65–190	35		42–43	50	120
Bruichladdich – 21-year-old (53.4%)	53	190		85			
Bruichladdich – 21-year-old – 1965 (43%)							110
Bruichladdich – 21-year-old – 1965 (G & M, 53.5%)						60	

Whisky Auction Sale Results (£s)	2000	2001	2002	2003	2004	2005	2006
Bruichladdich – 21-year-old – 1967 (43%)					120		
Bruichladdich – 21-year-old – 1972 (53.4%)				100			
Bruichladdich – 22-year-old – 1965 (Italian import, 48.8%)	115–200	90					
Bruichladdich – 23-year-old – 1978 (51%)						35	
Bruichladdich – 25-year-old – 1965 (G & M, 53.5%)						80	
Bruichladdich – 25-year-old (45%)	30	28–45	40				
Bruichladdich Stillman's Dram – 25-year-old 45%)							62
Bruichladdich Stillman's Dram – 26-year-old (45%)						60	
Bruichladdich Stillman's Dram – 27-year-old (45%)						45	
Bruichladdich – 28-year-old – 1968 (Signatory, 49.6%)				45			
Bruichladdich – 28-year-old – 1970 (50%)	55						50
Bruichladdich – 30-year-old – 1969 (Cadenhead's, 46.5%)					70–74		

Left to right.
Bruichladdich – 10 year-old,
Bruichladdich

Whisky Auction Sale Results (£s)	2000	2001	2002	2003	2004	2005	2006
Bruichladdich – 30-year-old – 1973 (40.2%)						80	
Bruichladdich – 32-year-old – 1967 (Signatory, 48%)	80	80					
Bruichladdich – 32-year-old – 1967 (First Cask, 46%)					40–50	42	
Bruichladdich – 32-year-old – 1967 (Signatory, 47.7%)		90					
Bruichladdich Legacy Series IV – 32-year-old (47.5%)							150
Bruichladdich – 35-year-old – 1966 (Old Malt Cask, 40.5%)		80					60
Bruichladdich – 35-year-old – 1966 (Hart Bros, 44.5%)			40		43		
Bruichladdich Legacy Series I – 36-year-old (40.6%)					110	100–110	110
Bruichladdich Legacy Series II – 37-year-old (41.8%)					160	110	
Bruichladdich – 1964 (G & M, half)					76		
Bruichladdich – 1970 (44.2%)						90	75–100
Bruichladdich Valinich – 1970 (45.5%)						35	
Bruichladdich Valinich – 1970 (47.3%)			50				200
Bruichladdich – 1970 (45.8%)						30–35	
Bruichladdich – 1979 (SMWS, 55.4%)							70
Bruichladdich Valinch – 1972 (48.8%)				65		53–77	
Bruichladdich – 1974 (SMWS, 57%)		189					
Bruichladdich – 1981 (SMWS, 58.6%)					50		
Bruichladdich Valinich – 1983 (58.8%)						53	80
Bruichladdich – 1984 (46%)						50	40
Bruichladdich Valinch – 1986 (53.5%)				65		77	80
Bruichladdich Valinch – 1988 (59.9%)							100
Bruichladdich Valinch – 1990 (60.2%)					63		40

Bunnahabhain

Only a few examples of Bunnahabhain have appeared at auction so far, the cask strength examples of this fine Islay malt represent excellent value

Whisky Auction Sale Results (£s)	2000	2001	2002	2003	2004	2005	2006
Bunnahabhain Moine (59.6%)					140–190	130	
Bunnahabhain Port Wood – 12-year-old (53.4%)							60
Bunnahabhain – 12-year-old (75 cl.)			20	47	16–70	33–40	30
Bunnahabhain – 17-year-old – 1965 (G & M)							130
Bunnahabhain – 19-year-old – 1980 (First Cask)					40–50	42	
Bunnahabhain – 20-year-old – 1979 (Murray McDavid, 46%)							45
Bunnahabhain – 24-year-old – 1979 (Cadenhead's, 50.6%)					35	40	40
Bunnahabhain – 1963 (43%)	30	50	45–55		150	60	160

Left to righ. Bunnahabhain – 1965, Bunnahabhain – 1966, Bunnahabhain Auld Aquantance – 1968, Bunnahabhain – 1963

Whisky Auction Sale Results (£s)	2000	2001	2002	2003	2004	2005	2006
Bunnahabhain – 22-year-old – 1978 (Signatory, 43%)							35
Bunnahabhain – 25-year-old – 1964 (Signatory, 46%)					70		
Bunnahabhain – 1965 (G & M, 40%)					51–115		
Bunnahabhain – 35-year-old – 1965 (53.9%)		180	150	160–200	160–220	165–200	180–200
Bunnahabhain – 35-year-old – 1966 (46.1%)				140–160	170–180	210–225	170–200
Bunnahabhain – 35-year-old – 1967 (43.8%)					180		
Bunnahabhain – 35-year-old – 1966 (Hart Bros, 43.2%)			62				
Bunnahabhain – 35-year-old – 1967 (Hart Bros, 40.5%)					62		58
Bunnahabhain – 38-year-old – 1960 (Old Malt Cask, 43.6%)	80		120				
Bunnahabhain – 39-year-old – 1960 (Old Malt Cask, 43.4%)			120				190
Bunnahabhain – 40-year-old – 1963 (42.9%)					200–230		
Bunnahabhain Auld Aquantance – 1968 (43.8%)					95–135	105	130–160
Bunnahabhain – The Family Silver – 1968			30–50		50	42–68	65–80
Bunnahabhain – 1974 (SMWS, 57.1%)		167					
Bunnahabhain – 1975 (SMWS, 57%)					50		
Bunnahabhain – 1979 (SMWS, 54.1%)					33		

Cambus

Only a small selection of Single Grain whisky from Cambus has made an appearance at auction so far largely due to the fact that only a limited amount of spirit has ever been bottled for re-sale

Whisky Auction Sale Results (£s)	2000	2001	2002	2003	2004	2005	2006
Old Cambus – 1891 – 13-year-old (Matthew Gloag)	1350						
Cambus (United Distillers, 75 cl., 40%)				130			
Cambus – 13-year-old (63.6%)	75						
Cambus – 15-year-old (63%)	75	33					
Cambus – 31-year-old – 1963 (Cadenhead's, 53.2%)					45–95		

Cameronbridge

These are the only three expressions of Single Grain whisky from Cameronbridge, bottled by Signatory and Cadenhead's, that have been sold at auction recently

Whisky Auction Sale Results (£s)	2000	2001	2002	2003	2004	2005	2006
Cameronbridge – 44-year-old – 1950 (42%)	230						
Cameronbridge – 30-year-old – 1954 (Cadenhead's, 46%)					90		
Cameronbridge – 35-year-old – 1959 (53.2%)			120				

Cameronbridge – 30-year-old – 1954
(Cadenhead's)

Caol Ila

The Caol Ila Manager's Dram, 150th Anniversary and early distillery bottlings are among the most sought after and fetch healthy prices

Whisky Auction Sale Results (£s)	2000	2001	2002	2003	2004	2005	2006
Caol Ila – 10-year-old – 1993 (Hart Bros, 57.3%)					31	20–22	
Caol Ila – 11-year-old – 1988 (Adelphi, 58.5%)							23
Caol Ila – 11-year-old – 1991 (Cadenhead's, 43%)						29	
Caol Ila – 12-year-old (Bulloch Lade & Co)	180–420	410	120–140	160	135–165	140–180	
Caol Ila – 12-year-old – 1969 (G & M)					160		
Caol Ila – 12-year-old – 1978 (Cadenhead's, 45.7%)							160–200
Caol Ila – 12-year-old – 1979 (Bristol Brandy Co., 43%)				47			
Caol Ila – 14-year-old (Italian import)		180–190					
Caol Ila – 15-year-old (Italian import)						70	
Caol Ila – 14-year-old – 1969 (G & M)			80			170–175	
Caol Ila – 15-year-old – 1969 (G & M)			110				
Caol Ila – 15-year-old – 1972 (G & M)					160	140	
Caol Ila – 15-year-old (Flora & Fauna)	38		30–33	27–35	35–55	30–47	20–70
Caol Ila – 15-year-old (Bulloch Lade & Co)		300				250	
Caol Ila – 15-year-old (Ceramic jug)	220				90	125–140	
Caol Ila – 15-year-old (Manager's Dram)	175–390	270–440	260–300	250	280	310–330	300–360
Caol Ila – 1965 (G & M, 45.6%)							130
Caol Ila – 1966 (G & M, Centenary Reserve)		120–160			80–130		
Caol Ila – 1969 (G & M, 45%)						120	
Caol Ila – 16-year-old – 1969 (G & M)	43		90–125		150		
Caol Ila – 16-year-old – 1972 (G & M)	58				160		

Whisky Auction Sale Results (£s)	2000	2001	2002	2003	2004	2005	2006
Caol Ila – 1972 (G & M)							50
Caol Ila – 16-year-old – 1977 (Cadenhead's, 64.3%)						155	
Caol Ila – 17-year-old – 1969 (G & M)		90					
Caol Ila – 17-year-old – 1966 (Cadenhead's, 46%)							310
Caol Ila – 18-year-old – 1974 (Prestonfield House)		155					
Caol Ila – 18-year-old – 1974 (First Cask)					30		
Caol Ila – 19-year-old – 1974 (First Cask)		50			39–60		50
Caol Ila – 20-year-old (150th Anniversary, 57.8%)	220–330	210–250	150–260	200–280	200–220	180–300	400
Caol Ila – 20-year-old (150th Anniversary, in presentation case with water jug)		440					
Caol Ila – 20-year-old – 1975 (61.1%)	36	40	36–55	27–50	25–57	65	60–65
Caol Ila – 20-year-old – 1977			60				
Caol Ila – 20-year-old – 1978 (61.18%)							100
Caol Ila – 21-year-old – 1981 (First Cask)					30–52		
Caol Ila – 21-year-old – 1975 (61.3%)	47	53	36			55	
Caol Ila – 22-year-old – 1974 (Signatory, 43%)					25		
Caol Ila – 22-year-old – 1975 (Hart Bros)	47				37		

Left to right.
Caol Ila Manager's Dram – 15-year-old,
Caol Ila Cask Strength – 1981

Whisky Auction Sale Results (£s)	2000	2001	2002	2003	2004	2005	2006
Caol Ila – 23-year-old – 1974 (First Cask)					55	110	
Caol Ila – 23-year-old – 1978 (61.7%)						45	60
Caol Ila – 25-year-old – 1979 (Douglas Laing, 50%)						50	30–50
Caol Ila – 25-year-old (59.4%)						50	60–80
Caol Ila – 1974 (G & M, 40%)							30
Caol Ila – 26-year-old – 1977 (Douglas Laing, 57.7%)							80
Caol Ila – 1975 (G & M, 40%)			47	27–40			
Caol Ila – 1977 (G & M, 40%)					57–67	65	60
Caol Ila – 1977 (Blackadder, 60.8%)	39						
Caol Ila – 1978 (Italian import, 46%)			122				
Caol Ila – 1978 (Cadenhead's. 64.7%)				63			
Caol Ila – 1978 (G & M, 40%)				25	35–80		
Caol Ila – 1980 (G & M, 65.3%)			60			53	
Caol Ila – 1980 (G & M, 40%)						55	
Caol Ila – 1981 (63.8%)	50–60	70			70	47	85
Caol Ila – 1981 (G & M, 40%)	46–47			30–45			
Caol Ila – 1984 (G & M, 46%)	47						
Caol Ila – 1984 (G & M, 40%)			37			27–60	
Caol Ila – 1988 (G & M, 40%)						40	
Caol Ila – 1988 (G & M, 57.6%)						40	
Caol Ila Calvados Wood Finish – 1988 (G & M)		38					22–23
Caol Ila Cognac Wood Finish – 1988 (G & M)		38			30		15–23
Caol Ila Claret Wood Finish – 1988 (G & M)		38			30		23
Caol Ila – 1991 (G & M, 57.4%)							30
Caol Ila – 1993 (G & M, 57.8%)							30

Caperdonich

This small though interesting selection of Caperdonich has been sold with success at auction recently and the presence of malt from the distillery continues to be represented

Whisky Auction Sale Results (£s)	2000	2001	2002	2003	2004	2005	2006
Caperdonich – 5-year-old (75 cl.)				72			
Caperdonich – 11-year-old – 1968 (G & M)			75			70	
Caperdonich – 12-year-old – 1965 (Cadenhead's)		100	82				
Caperdonich – 14-year-old – 1965 (Cadenhead's, 45.7%)					95		
Caperdonich – 14-year-old – 1968 (G & M)					80–110		
Caperdonich – 17-year-old – 1968 (G & M)			75				
Caperdonich – 16-year-old – 1972 (Signatory, 40%)				25	40	80	
Caperdonich – 30-year-old – 1966 (Signatory, 53.4%)						80	
Caperdonich – 30-year-old – 1968 (Signatory, 50.3%)		180					
Caperdonich – 32-year-old – 1968 (Hart Bros, 44.5%)			32		48	30	40–45
Caperdonich – 35-year-old – 1965 (Cadenhead's, 47.2%)					80		
Caperdonich – 35-year-old – 1968 (Mission Series 3, 46%)							42
Caperdonich – 1968 (G & M, 40%)			30–40		33–37		50
Caperdonich – 1974 (SMWS, 60.1%)					50		
Caperdonich – 1979 (G & M, 40%)					25		
Caperdonich – 1980 (G & M, 40%)	27		22–26		35–90	25	32
Caperdonich – 1980 (SMWS, 61.2%)		67					

Cardhu

The Cardhu Manager's Dram shows a very healthy growth over recent years and early distillery bottlings have proved to be sought after among collectors, particularly those labelled under the Cardow distillery name

Whisky Auction Sale Results (£s)	2000	2001	2002	2003	2004	2005	2006
Cardow (Stopper cork, 70 degrees proof)					650	820	
Cardow – 16-year-old – 1962 (Cadenhead's, 45.7%)						300	300
Cardhu – 12-year-old (Tall, 75 cl.)	70	100	55–100	70–100	45–130		120
Cardhu – 12-year-old (Square, dumpy, 75 cl.)				37–96	25–60	35–45	32–55
Cardhu – 12-year-old (Square, dumpy, 70 cl.)							27–37
Cardhu – 12-year-old (Square, dumpy, litre)					37		27
Cardhu – 12-year-old (Tall, litre)			110	100	50–60		
Cardhu – 15-year-old (Manager's Dram)	175–230		150–260	145–170	180	230	230
Cardhu – 25-year-old – 1974 (Signatory, 56%)					60–65	90	
Cardhu – 27-year-old – 1973 (60.02%)							95

Left to right.
Cardow, Cardow (Cadenhead's),
Cardhu – 12-year-old,
Cardhu Manager's Dram – 15-year-old

Carsebridge

These are the only examples of Single Grain whisky from Carsebridge, bottled by Hart Bros, Signatory and Chieftain's Choice that have been sold at auction recently, probably one of very few bottlings ever released

Whisky Auction Sale Results (&s)	2000	2001	2002	2003	2004	2005	2006
Carsedridge – 40-year-old – 1965 (Hart Bros, 46.5%)							60–70
Carsedridge – 43-year-old – 1960 (Chieftain's, 41.6%)							160
Carsebridge – 28-year-old – 1965 (57.8%)			100				

Clynelish

The Clynelish Manager's Dram has been very popular over recent years, cask strength Clynelish is very popular too, equally older distillery bottlings are much sought after by collectors as also is the spirit of Free Embo bottling

Whisky Auction Sale Results (£s)	2000	2001	2002	2003	2004	2005	2006
Clynelish – 5-year-old (Ainslie & Heilbron)		90–180					
Clynelish – 9-year-old – 1989 (Adelphi, 61.6%)			30	25			
Clynelish – 12-year-old (Ainslie & Heilbron, 75 cl.)	60		65–115	75–160	80–130	60–115	95–190
Clynelish – 12-year-old (Ainslie & Heilbron, Italian export, 56.9%)	120–170	130–150					
Clynelish – 12-year-old Spirit of Free Embo				420	220	350	
Clynelish – 12-year-old – 1982 (Cadenhead's, 65.4%)						38	
Clynelish – 12-year-old – 1990 (Coopers Choice, 43%)							25
Clynelish – 14-year-old (Flora & Fauna)	38		23–30	20–48	27–50	25	38–70

Clynelish Spirit of Free Embo – 12-year-old

Whisky Auction Sale Results (£s)	2000	2001	2002	2003	2004	2005	2006
Clynelish – 14-year-old – 1990 (Douglas of Drumlanrig, 45%)							30
Clynelish – 16-year-old – 1984 (Adelphi, 54%)							22
Clynelish – 17-year-old (Manager's Dram)	130–175	83–128	40–98	60–135	80–85	60–85	80–125
Clynelish – 20-year-old – 1983 (46%)						48	42
Clynelish – 23-year-old – 1972 (57%)	25		50			63	67
Clynelish – 23-year-old – 1974 (59.1%)				37	33–62		
Clynelish – 24-year-old – 1972 (61.3%)		47			57	42–80	100
Clynelish – 24-year-old (Ainslie & Heilbron, Italian export, 49.4%)	145						
Clynelish – 28-year-old – 1965 (Signatory, 50.7%)	125			70			
Clynelish – 28-year-old – 1965 (Signatory, 50.7% with 2 miniatures)	450						
Clynelish – 28-year-old – 1976 (Mission Series 4, 46%)							40
Clynelish – 29-year-old – 1965 (Signatory, 52.1%)		180	88	80	95		
Clynelish – 30-year-old – 1970 (D. McGibbon, 45.4%)						40	
Clynelish – 30-year-old – 1972 (Mission Sel. 1, 46%)							40
Clynelish – 1982 (SMWS, 64.5%)		67					
Clynelish – 1982 (57.7%)					35		

Coleburn

A few bottlings of Coleburn have come up at auction in recent years, those that have are mainly cask strength examples

Whisky Auction Sale Results (£s)	2000	2001	2002	2003	2004	2005	2006
Coleburn – 1972 (G & M)	28–46		37	25–35	35–43	24	33–45
Coleburn – 1981 (SMWS, 65.3%)					60		
Coleburn – 12-year-old – 1968 (G & M)							65
Coleburn – 14-year-old – 1983 (Signatory, 43%)						30	
Coleburn – 16-year-old – 1983 (Signatory, 43%)				32			
Coleburn – 17-year-old – 1965 (G & M)				50	80	80–90	
Coleburn – Glenlivet – 17-year-old – 1978 (Cadenhead's, 62%)			40			50	
Coleburn – 18-year-old – 1981 (Signatory, 46%)							20
Coleburn – 19-year-old – 1981 (Signatory, 43%)				37			
Coleburn – 21-year-old – 1979 (59.4%)			105	50	90		
Coleburn – 28-year-old – 1971 (Old Malt Cask, 50%)				45			
Coleburn – 29-year-old – 1970 (Old Malt Cask, 50%)	45–55						70
Coleburn – 34 year-old – 1967 (Old Malt Cask, 50.4%)						60–110	
Coleburn – 35-year-old – 1964 (The Bottlers, 46.9%)	130				60		

Convalmore

These expressions of Convalmore that have been sold at auction recently are independent bottlings mainly at cask strength

Whisky Auction Sale Results (£s)	2000	2001	2002	2003	2004	2005	2006
Convalmore – 12-year-old – 1969 (G & M)		90		60			
Convalmore – 13-year-old – 1969 (G & M)						85	
Convalmore – 1969 (G & M, 40%)						37	
Convalmore – 16-year-old – 1962 (Cadenhead's, 45.7%)	130		70		100	150	100
Convalmore – 16-year-old – 1981 (First Cask)		20–24			32	24	
Convalmore – 16-year-old – 1981 (43%)				37			
Convalmore – 1969 (G & M)		38	32–45	32–37	35–40	37	
Convalmore – Glenlivet – 20-year-old – 1977 (Cadenhead's, 65.2%)			40				
Convalmore – Glenlivet – 23-year-old – 1962 (Cadenhead's, 92 US proof)							105
Convalmore – 23-year-old – 1976 (Silent Stills)	52						
Convalmore – 24-year-old – 1976 (Signatory, 43%)				25			
Convalmore – Glenlivet – 30-year-old – 1962 (Cadenhead's, 46.5%)				85	60		
Convalmore – 36-year-old – 1960 (G & M, 40%)				120			
Convalmore – 36-year-old – 1961 (G & M, 40%)							70
Convalmore – 1981 (G & M)	28						30–32
Convalmore – 1981 (Spirit of Scotland, 40%)					37		

Cragganmore

The Cragganmore is another highly popular Manager's Dram, older bottlings by Gordon & MacPhail can be difficult to find

Whisky Auction Sale Results (£s)	2000	2001	2002	2003	2004	2005	2006
Cragganmore – 11-year-old – 1968 (G & M, 70 degrees)			75	150			
Cragganmore – 12-year-old (75cl, 43%)	25						35
Cragganmore – 12-year-old (Litre)							27
Cragganmore – 12-year-old (D & J McCalllum, 75 cl. 45.7%)				97–120	33		
Cragganmore – 12-year-old (59.3%)							90
Cragganmore – 12-year-old – 1968 (G & M)							70
Cragganmore – 14-year-old (Classic Malts, 47.5%)			33–38				53
Cragganmore – 14-year-old – 1971 (G & M, 40%)			65				

Left to right.
Convalmore – Glenlivet – 16-year-old (Cadenhead's),
Cragganmore Manager's Dram – 17-year-old

Whisky Auction Sale Results (&s)	2000	2001	2002	2003	2004	2005	2006
Cragganmore – 14-year-old – 1972 (G & M, 40%)					100		
Cragganmore – 15-year-old – 1972 (G & M, 40%)		90–100					
Cragganmore – 17-year-old (Manager's Dram)	230	95–195	55–125	95–100	105–110	90–100	100–130
Cragganmore-Glenlivet – 18-year-old – 1961 (Cadenhead's, 46%)					115		160
Cragganmore – 1972 (G & M, 56.5%)					65		
Cragganmore – 1972 (SMWS, 55.8%)						60	
Cragganmore – 1974 (SMWS, 58.8%)		167					
Cragganmore – 1976 (G & M, 40%)	43						
Cragganmore – 1977 (G & M, 40%)				37			
Cragganmore – 1984 (Distiller's Edition, 40%)			27			35	
Cragganmore – 1985 (Distiller's Edition, 40%)							30
Cragganmore – 1987 (Distiller's Edition, 43%)							23
Cragganmore – 1988 (Distiller's Edition, 40%)							47
Cragganmore – 1990 (Distiller's Edition, 40%)							32

Craigellachie

These are a few examples to illustrate the popularity of this Speyside malt, the rarest being the Centenary bottling sold in 2003

Whisky Auction Sale Results (£s)	2000	2001	2002	2003	2004	2005	2006
Craigellachie – 12-year-old – 1971 (G & M, 40%)				60			
Craigellachie – 13-year-old – 1971 (G & M, 40%)						90	90
Craigellachie Centenary – 14-year-old (Flora & Fauna)				360			
Craigellachie – 14-year-old (Flora & Fauna)	38		20–30	35–48	27–40		38–70
Craigellachie – 14-year-old – 1971 (G & M)	57						
Craigellachie – 14-year-old – 1980 (Signatory)			28				
Craigellachie – 15-year-old – 1984 (Hart Bros)		27					
Craigellachie – 16-year-old – 1978 (First Cask)		20			34	23	25
Craigellachie – Glenlivet – 19-year-old – 1962							
(Cadenhead's, 46%)						110	
Craigellachie – 22-year-old – 1973 (60.2%)		35		32–35		30–47	57
Craigellachie – 33-year-old – 1970 (46%)						60	42
Craigellachie – Glenlivet – 37-year-old – 1962							
(Cadenhead's, 48.2%)		180	85		100		
Craigellachie – 1973 (SMWS, 53.6%)		50					
Craigellachie – 1974 (G & M, 40%)			25–37	21	31–40	30	31
Craigellachie – 1988 (G & M, 40%)							45

Dailuaine

The Dailuaine Manager's Dram and cask strength Rare Malts expressions have had the most exposure at auction to date

Whisky Auction Sale Results (£s)	2000	2001	2002	2003	2004	2005	2006
Dailuaine – 1962 (R W Duthie, Italian import, 46%)	85						
Dailuaine – 13-year-old – 1966 (Cadenhead's, 45.7%)						160	150
Dailuaine – 14-year-old – 1971 (G & M, 75 cl.)					70		
Dailuaine – 1971 (G & M, 75 cl.)			20–60		43–45	26	
Dailuaine – 1974 (G & M)				30		20	31
Dailuaine – 1975 (SMWS, 57.3%)					65		
Dailuaine – 1980 (63%)	30					45	37–50
Dailuaine – 16-year-old (Flora & Fauna)	38		20–30	20–32	20–35		
Dailuanie – 17-year-old (Manager's Dram)		90–180	50–80		70–105	68	55–95
Dailuaine – 17-year-old – 1980 (Hart Bros)		20					
Dailuaine – 18-year-old – 1963 (G & M)						80	
Dailuaine – 21-year-old – 1980 (Adelphi, 56.1%)							20
Dailuaine – 22-year-old – 1962 (Cadenhead's, 46%)							95
Dailuaine – 22-year-old – 1973 (60.92%)	36–45	35–43	47	40	30–62		60–85
Dailuaine – 27-year-old – 1952 (Cadenhead's, 50.8%)			190	160			
Dailuaine – Glenlivet – 27-year-old – 1962 (Cadenhead's, 50.8%)		90					
Dailuaine – 27-year-old – 1973 (First Cask, 46%)					28		
Dailuaine – 30-year-old – 1973 (First Cask)							45
Dailuaine – Glenlivet – 31-year-old – 1966 (Cadenhead's, 56.8%)					90		

Whisky Auction Sale Results (£s)	2000	2001	2002	2003	2004	2005	2006
Dailuaine – 40-year-old – 1962 (Douglas Laing, 46.3%)					80	90–100	90

Dailuaine Manager's Dram –
17-year-old

Dalaruan

This rare early 20th century example is the only historical bottling from Dalaruan distillery that has been sold at auction over the last decade

Whisky Auction Sale Results (£s)	2000	2001	2002	2003	2004	2005	2006
Dalaruan Special Reserve – 1901		4200					

Left to right.
Dalaruan – 1901,
Dallas Dhu – 16-year-old (Cadenhead's)

Dallas Dhu

A varied selection of bottlings from Dallas Dhu have appeared at auction in recent years

Whisky Auction Sale Results (£s)	2000	2001	2002	2003	2004	2005	2006
Dallas Dhu – 10-year-old (G & M, 75 cl.)					20–37	34–53	
Dallas Dhu – 12-year-old (G & M)							38
Dallas Dhu – 14-year-old – 1968 (G & M)					80		
Dallas Dhu – 15-year-old – 1969 (G & M)	43						
Dallas Dhu – 15-year-old – 1978 (First Cask, 46%)				70		50	
Dallas Dhu – 16-year-old – 1969 (G & M)				100	100	95	
Dallas Dhu – 16-year-old – 1962 (Cadenhead's, 47.7%)		160			135		210
Dallas Dhu – 16-year-old – 1971 (G & M)			110		100		
Dallas Dhu – 16-year-old – 1980 (Signatory, 43%)						29	
Dallas Dhu – 17-year-old – 1970 (G & M)			80				85
Dallas Dhu – 17-year-old – 1974 (Signatory, 43%)						47	
Dallas Dhu – 18-year-old – 1970 (G & M)						105	
Dallas Dhu – 18-year-old – 1974 (Signatory, 43%)					43		
Dallas Dhu – 18-year-old – 1978 (Silent Stills)				65			
Dallas Dhu – 21-year-old – 1962 (Cadenhead's, 46%)					60		
Dallas Dhu – 20-year-old – 1977 (First Cask)					32	50	
Dallas Dhu – 21-year-old – 1975 (61.9%)	47			35–45	50–67	25–60	25–65
Dallas Dhu – 22-year-old – 1962 (A Mackay & Co, 92 USA Proof)		320			170		
Dallas Dhu – 22-year-old – 1978 (Signatory, 59.7%)							55
Dallas Dhu – 23-year-old – 1974 (First Cask)		60					

Whisky Auction Sale Results (£s)	2000	2001	2002	2003	2004	2005	2006
Dallas Dhu – 23-year-old – 1974 (Signatory, 59.8%)						50–60	
Dallas Dhu – 23-year-old – 1978 (Signatory, 46%)					80		
Dallas Dhu – 23-year-old – 1978 (Signatory, 43%)							45
Dallas Dhu – 23-year-old – 1979 (Mission Ser. 1, 46%)							30–40
Dallas Dhu – 24-year-old – 1970 (60.6%)	36–55	57	53		37–83	62–107	
Dallas Dhu – 24-year-old – 1970 (60.54%)			80	72			
Dallas Dhu – 24-year-old – 1979 (First Cask)					50		
Dallas Dhu Millennium – 25-year-old – 1974 (43%)			90–100	110		75–100	
Dallas Dhu – 26-year-old (Cadenhead's, 44.5%)						105–115	
Dallas Dhu – 29-year-old – 1974 (46%)						50	42
Dallas Dhu – 30-year-old – 1970 (Signatory, 56.5%)		70					
Dallas Dhu – 31-year-old – 1970 (Douglas Laing)						55	
Dallas Dhu – 32-year-old – 1970 (Cooper's Choice, 46%)						50	
Dallas Dhu – 1970 (Italian import, crystal decanter)		170					
Dallas Dhu – 1971 (G & M, 75 cl.)				27		57	35
Dallas Dhu – 1972 (G & M, 75 cl.)	58		60			34–42	
Dallas Dhu – 1973 (G & M, 75 cl.)						41–42	
Dallas Dhu – 1975 (SMWS, 58.5%)		167					
Dallas Dhu – 1975 (SMWS, 61.1%)			47				
Dallas Dhu – 1979 (G & M, 70 cl.)			40			25–50	45
Dallas Dhu – 1980 (G & M, 70 cl.)						27	
Dallas Dhu Centenary (Cask 262, 40%)			170			75–80	125
Dallas Dhu Last Cask Filled – 1983 (48%)	150	150	270	140		170	190–200

Dalmore

The sale at auction of The Dalmore Kildermorie – 62-year-old in 2002 broke the world record for a single bottle of Single Malt whisky when it fetched £22,000 which at the time of this publication going to press was still unbroken. The 1980s release of Dalmore – 50-year-old represents excellent value for such a rare and mature single malt, the crystal decanter of 30-year-old is highly sought after and the old bottlings of younger spirit are very popular too

Whisky Auction Sale Results (£s)	2000	2001	2002	2003	2004	2005	2006
Dalmore – 62-year-old – The Kildermorie bottle (Vatting of 1868, 1878, 1926 & 1939, Dalmore, 40.5%)			22,000				
Dalmore – 8-year-old (D MacBeth & Co, 75 cl.)		70					180–190
Dalmore – Over-8-year-old (Mackenzie Bros)						215	
Dalmore – 10-year-old (Whyte & MacKay for Marks & Spencer, 40%)				47			
Dalmore – 11-year-old – 1989 (Adelphi, 57.2%)							20

Left to right. Dalmore – 50-year-old-1926, Dalmore – 25-year-old-Pre 1960, Dalmore – 8-year-old (Mackenzie Bros)

THE
DALMORE™

AGED **62** YEARS

Single Highland Malt
SCOTCH WHISKY

ON THE 4TH DECEMBER 2002,
ONE OF ONLY 12 BOTTLES
PRODUCED SOLD FOR
£25,877.50, SETTING A NEW
WORLD RECORD FOR THE
MOST EXPENSIVE WHISKY.

WHEN YOU DISCOVER THE
SENSATIONAL STORY OF
THIS **62 YEAR OLD TREASURE**
AND HOW IT HAS BEEN
LOVINGLY FORGED FROM
THE HIGHLANDS OF
SCOTLAND, YOU REALISE
THIS IS A **MASTERPIECE
WORTHY OF ITS TITLE**

This is brilliant: pure silk wrapping
fabulous moist fruitcake soaked
in finest Oloroso sherry and then
weighed with peat which somehow
has defied nature and survived in
cask all these years. I really cannot
fault this: I sit here stunned in
awe…A once-in-a-lifetime whisky…

Jim Murray's Whisky Bible 2005

Should you wish to learn more about
our other rare whiskies please email
rare@whyteandmackay.com

Whisky Auction Sale Results (£s)	2000	2001	2002	2003	2004	2005	2006
Dalmore – 12-year-old (D MacBeth & Co)	70–80		75	160			
Dalmore – 12-year-old (Whyte & MacKay, 75 cl.)	35–45		35–45	37–70	40–75	43	80
Dalmore – 12-year-old (Forming of Kyndal, 2001)						100–110	50
Dalmore – 20-year-old (Italian Anniversary bottling, Whyte & MacKay)	110–140		125				
Dalmore – 20-year-old (D MacBeth & Co)	120	140					
Dalmore – 20-year-old (Mackenzie Bros)		320					300–360
Dalmore – 25-year-old – Pre 1960 (Whyte & MacKay)				270			
Dalmore – 1985 (SMWS, 57.5%)						60	
Dalmore – 1979 (SMWS, 64.9%)			47				
Dalmore – 1979 (SMWS, 65.8%)					70		
Dalmore – 28-year-old – 1974 (57.9%)						150	
Dalmore – 30-year-old (Stillman's Dram, 45%)				290			
Dalmore – 30-year-old – 1959 (Crystal decanter)		1400		1000–1150	1400		
Dalmore – 30-year-old – 1963 (Cadenhead's, 54.5%)				90			
Dalmore – 30-year-old – 1966 (Shepherd Neame, 50%)						210	
Dalmore – 30-year-old – 1973 (42%)						105	
Dalmore – 40-year-old – 1964 (Crystal decanter, John Doig Memorial decanter, 45%)					950		
Dalmore – 30-year-old – 1966 (Limited release, 50%)		220					
Dalmore – 50-year-old – 1926 (Ceramic decanter)	750		740–950	700–720	900	1100–1150	720–1250
Dalmore – 50-year-old – 1926 (Lacking case, seal cracked)						620	
Dalmore – 50-year-old (Crystal decanter, 52%)					2500		3100

Dalwhinnie

These are the only expressions of Dalwhinnie that have been sold at auction recently, the Centenary bottlings being the most frequently offered

Whisky Auction Sale Results (£s)	2000	2001	2002	2003	2004	2005	2006
Dalwhinnie – 8-year-old (Tall 75 cl.)							120–210
Dalwhinnie – 15-year-old (James Buchanan & Co, 75cl.)				37	30		105
Dalwhinnie Centenary – 15-year-old (56.1%)	200–220	140–190		55	45	105	
Dalwhinne – 15-year-old (56.9%)						30	53–60
Dalwhinnie Centenary – 15-year-old (Classic Malts, 56.9%)		40	35–55	30	25–50	28	25–60
Dalwhinnie – 22-year-old – 1957 (Cadenhead's, 45.7%)			80				140
Dalwhinnie – 20-year-old – 1963 (G & M)					100		
Dalwhinnie – 36-year-old – 1966 (47.2%)						200–220	
Dalwhinnie – 17-year-old – 1970 (G & M)		70	80				
Dalwhinnie Double Matured – 1980						35	
Dalwhinnie Double Matured – 1981	40		20	20			30
Dalwhinnie Double Matured – 1989							25–32

Dalwhinnie (Cadenhead's)

Deanston

These examples of Deanston listed are the only ones that have appeared at auction recently

Whisky Auction Sale Results (£s)	2000	2001	2002	2003	2004	2005	2006
Deanston Mill (26 2/3 fl. ozs.)			45–55	60		90	90
Deanston Mill – 5-year-old (Italian import)		125					
Deanston Mill – Over-8-year-old (75 cl.)						70	30
Deanston – Over-8-year-old	43		25–27		26–50		
Deanston – 25-year-old				40			
Deanston – 35-year-old – 1967 (50.7%)							140

Deanston – 8-year-old

Dufftown

Old expressions of Dufftown are becoming scarce now and make the occasional appearance at auction

Whisky Auction Sale Results (£s)	2000	2001	2002	2003	2004	2005	2006
Dufftown – Glenlivet – 8-year-old (Arthur Bell & Sons)	80	100–140	40–60	50–100	30–90	46–90	60–67
Dufftown – Glenlivet – 10-year-old (Arthur Bell & Sons)			35–47	47	30		
Dufftown – Glenlivet – 12-year-old (Arthur Bell & Sons)						45	
Dufftown – Glenivet – 14-year-old – 1966 Cadenhead's, 46%)							65
Dufftown – 15-year-old (Flora & Fauna)	38		20	27–48			37–50
Dufftown – 17-year-old (James MacArthur, 58.5%)						45	
Dufftown – Glenlivet Centenary – 20-year-old	310–420	150–420	80–130	80	80		65
Dufftown – Glenlivet Centenary – 20-year-old (Label damaged)		100					
Dufftown – Glenlivet – 21-year-old – 1958 (Cadenhead's, 45.7%)					80		
Dufftown – Glenlivet – 21-year-old – 1975 (54.8%)	36		36		30	42	45–180
Dufftown – Glenlivet – 28-year-old – 1966 (Cadenhead's 52.5%)			75				
Dufftown – Glenlivet – 1966 (Old Cadenhead's, bottled 1989, 52.5%)			130				
Dufftown – Glenlivet – 40-year-old		480					
Dufftown – 1979 (Cadenhead's, 59.1%)						67	
Dufftown – 1992 (59.6%)		20					

Edradour

These examples of Edradour listed are the only ones that have appeared at auction so far

Whisky Auction Sale Results (£s)	2000	2001	2002	2003	2004	2005	2006
Edradour – 10-year-old (Stone jug)	40					52	50
Edradour – 10-year-old (75 cl.)					32–52		
Edradour – 10-year-old – 1972 (G & M)					100		
Edradour – 10-year-old (Bottled for BBC Scotland *Children in Need*, 1986, 40%)				75			
Edradour – 10-year-old (Opening of distillery, 1986, 40%)				90			
Edradour – 11-year-old – 1991 (60.2%)						27	
Edradour – 18-year-old – 1976 (Cadenhead's, 51.7%)			37	45			
Edradour – 21-year-old – 1968 (Signatory, 46%)	62				70		37
Edradour – 1989 (Glass decanter, 58.2%)					30		
Edradour – 1989 (Glass decanter, 57.2%)						27	
Edradour – 11-year-old (Signatory glass decanter, 59.2%)					30		

Fettercairn

Only a small selection of Fettercairn has made an appearance at auction recently, the highlight being the Charles Doig decanter

Whisky Auction Sale Results (£s)	2000	2001	2002	2003	2004	2005	2006
Fettercairn Old Scotch Whisky – Early 20th century					210		
Fettercairn 875 – 8-year-old (Italian import)		85	150			100–110	
Fettercairn – Bonded – 1960				70			
Fettercairn – 12-year-old – 1965 (Cadenhead's)		100					
Old Fettercairn (26 2/3 fl. ozs.)	42–43		45–65	30–70	30–70	70	
Old Fettercairn – 8-year-old		100				110	70
Old Fettercairn – 10-year-old (75 cl.)	42		37	30		57	
Fettercairn – 21-year-old – 1957 (Cadenhead's, 45.7%)							190
Old Fettercairn Stillman's Dram – 26-year-old (45%)						37–60	
Fettercairn 1824 – 30-year-old (45%)						70	
Fettercairn – 30-year-old – Pre 1955 (41.2%)					220		
Fettercairn – 39-year-old – 1964 (Crystal decanter, Charles Doig Memorial, 45%)					850		

Fettercairn – 39-year-old-1964

COLLECTING MALT WHISKY – A PRICE GUIDE

Glen Albyn

These are the only expressions of Glen Albyn that have been sold at auction recently, those detailed include Cadenhead's, Gordon & MacPhail and Signatory bottlings

Whisky Auction Sale Results (£s)	2000	2001	2002	2003	2004	2005	2006
Glen Albyn – 10-year-old (J E McPherson & Son)	190					260	
Glen Albyn – 12-year-old – 1980 (Signatory, 43%)					27		
Glen Albyn – 15-year-old (Master of Malt, 43%)				32			
Glen Albyn – 15-year-old – 1963 (Cadenhead's, 45.7%)	130		60	65	110	120	115
Glen Albyn – 17-year-old – 1979 (Signatory, 43%)				25		30	
Glen Albyn – 19-year-old – 1963 (G & M)		110		110		120	115
Glen Albyn – 19-year-old – 1978 (Hart Bros, 43%)					25		
Glen Albyn – 21-year-old – 1963 (G & M)							105

*Glen Albyn – 15-year-old
(Cadenhead's)*

Whisky Auction Sale Results (£s)	2000	2001	2002	2003	2004	2005	2006
Glen Albyn – 23-year-old – 1965 (G & M)			130				
Glen Albyn – 25-year-old – 1964 (Signatory, 58%)	130				120		80
Glen Albyn – 26-year-old – 1974 (First Cask)					40		
Glen Albyn – 26-year-old – 1975 (54.8%)							50
Glen Albyn – 26-year-old – 1978 (Hart Bros, 47.5%)						25–32	
Glen Albyn – 30-year-old – 1964 (Cadenhead's, 46.7%)					80		
Glen Albyn – 31-year-old – 1965 (Silent Stills, 51.5%)	52				75	60	
Glen Albyn – 32-year-old – 1969 (Douglas Laing, 54.4%)							80
Glen Albyn – 1963 (G & M)			37				
Glen Albyn – 1965 (G & M)					40		
Glen Albyn – 1968 (G & M)			30–71	40	32–36		
Glen Albyn – 1972 (G & M)	22		22		42		30–60
Glen Albyn – 1974 (G & M)					37		
Glen Albyn – 1974 (Spirit of Scotland)					40–42		
Glen Albyn – 1975 (Cadenhead's, 65.4%)					100		
Glen Albyn – 1975 (Cadenhead's, 59.1%)					120	130	

Glen Elgin

Glen Elgin, The Manager's Drams, have been offered at auction quite frequently recently and fetched healthy prices

Whisky Auction Sale Results (£s)	2000	2001	2002	2003	2004	2005	2006
Glen Elgin (75 cl.)							33
Glen Elgin – 10-year-old – Early 20th Century						1300	
Glen Elgin – 12-year-old (White Horse Distillers Ltd)			70	35	42–100	80–135	40–100
Glen Elgin – 13-year-old – 1965 (Cadenhead's, 45.7%)							155
Glen Elgin – 14-year-old (Bottled by United Distillers, Christmas 1990, 43%)				520			
Glen Elgin – 15-year-old (Manager's Dram)		140–150	350	170–210	220	260–275	390
Glen Elgin – 16-year-old (Manager's Dram)	175–230	85–195	55–125	82–165	60–180	130–140	120–145
Glen Elgin Centenary – 19-year-old (60%)				140	120		90–130
Glen Elgin – 19-year-old – 1978 (Hart Bros, 43%)					38		
Glen Elgin – 1968 (G & M)				20		25–37	
Glen Elgin – 1971 (R W Duthie, 50%)		60					

Glen Elgin Manager's Dram – 16-year-old

Glenesk

The Glenesk Maltings – 25th Anniversary bottling has been highly sought after at auction recently and has fetched healthy figures

Whisky Auction Sale Results (£s)	2000	2001	2002	2003	2004	2005	2006
Glenesk (W Sanderson & Son, export)		400					260
Glenesk – 5-year-old (W Sanderson & Son)	75		60				
Glenesk – 12-year-old (W Sanderson & Son)	40		87		55–62	115	70
Glenesk Maltings – 1969 – 25th Anniversary	320	480–740	420–480	270–500		260	250–260
Glenesk – 26-year-old – 1974 (Signatory, 52.7%)					37		
Glen Esk – 31-year-old – 1970 (Douglas Laing, 56.9%)						100	
Glen Esk – 1979 (SMWS, 63.6%)							70
Glenesk – 1982 (G & M)		60	26	35	35	45	
Glenesk – 1984 (G & M)			37	20	26		
Glenesk – 1985 (G & M)				26	37	24	

Glen Grant

Some fine examples of Glen Grant have come up at auction, older expressions bottled by merchants attract great interest, likewise the wide and varied range of bottlings, the majority by Gordon & MacPhail spanning many years

Whisky Auction Sale Results (£s)	2000	2001	2002	2003	2004	2005	2006
Glen Grant – Believed late 19th century (J McWillam, Rothes)		1250					
Glen Grant – 1888 (R H Thomson & Co)	1900						
Glen Grant (75 cl.)						33	55
Glen Grant – 10-year-old (D Strachan Jnr.)						420	
Glen Grant – 1898 (W Proctor, Ballater)		1700					
Glen Grant – Early 20th century	1400						
Glen Grant – 1902 (Block, Grey & Block)		1550					
Glen Grant – 1903 (Morton, Dundee)		900					

Left to right.
Glen Grant – 1903 (Morton, Dundee),
Glen Grant – Early 20th Century,
Glen Grant (Hedges & Butler),
Glen Grant – 1933 (Baird Taylor)

Whisky Auction Sale Results (£s)	2000	2001	2002	2003	2004	2005	2006
Fine Old Glen Grant – Believed Circa 1950						150–160	
Guaranteed Fine Old Glen Grant						120	
Glen Grant – 32-year-old – 1919 (J Catto & Co)	980						
Glen Grant – 23-year-old – 1920 (Duncan MacLeod)		700					
Glen Grant – 1929 (Matthew Gloag & Son)	370					190	
Glen Grant – 1930 (Berry Bros & Rudd)		370					
Glen Grant – 1933 (W Baird Taylor, Glasgow)		880					
Glen Grant – 1936 (G & M)	250	320			260	290–320	
Glen Grant – 1949 (G & M)						130	
Glen Grant – 1950 (G & M)					100		
Glen Grant – 1952 (G & M)							125
Glen Grant – 1953 (G & M, 45%)							210
Glen Grant – 1956 (G & M)					80		
Glen Grant – 1957 (G & M)					80		
Glen Grant – 1957 (Berry Bros & Rudd)		110					
Glen Grant – 1958 (G & M)				65	70		210
Glen Grant – 1959 (G & M)					75		
Glen Grant – 1960 (G & M)	40				70		
Glen Grant – 5-year-old (Robert Watson, 100 proof)						140	
Glen Grant – 5-year-old (Peter Thomson, 26 2/3 fl. ozs.)							60–90
Glen Grant – 5-year-old – 1967	53		35	30	32		
Glen Grant – 5-year-old – 1968			40			25	
Glen Grant – 5-year-old – 1969							55
Glen Grant – 5-year-old – 1970			40		80		
Glen Grant – 5-year-old – 1971					32	25	

Whisky Auction Sale Results (£s)	2000	2001	2002	2003	2004	2005	2006
Glen Grant – 5-year-old – 1972					30		
Glen Grant – 5-year-old – 1973					30		
Glen Grant – 5-year-old – 1979		70					
Glen Grant – 5-year-old – 1980					25		
Glen Grant – 5-year-old – 1981					25		55
Glen Grant – 5-year-old – 1982					25		
Glen Grant – 5-year-old – 1983					25		
Glen Grant – 5-year-old – 1986					22		
Glen Grant – 5-year-old – 1987					20		
Glen Grant – 1980 (SMWS, 61%)					100		
Glen Grant – 8-year-old (Peter Thomson, Perth)				60–80	30		
Glen Grant – 8-year-old (Campbell, Hope & King, Securo screw cap)					210		
Glen Grant – 8-year-old (G & M, Securo screw cap)			170				
Glen Grant – 8-year-old (G & M, 26 2/3 fl. oz)				62			45
Glen Grant – 8-year-old (Half, Cadenhead's)	80						
Glen Grant – 8-year-old (Hall & Bramley)							60
Glen Grant – 10-year-old		45					
Glen Grant – 10-year-old (G & M, 26 2/3 fl. oz)				130	50		
Glen Grant – 10-year-old (W H Bauly Ltd)			100				
Glen Grant – 10-year-old (Hall & Bramley)				70			
Glen Grant – 10-year-old (G Strachan)		280					
Glen Grant – 12-year-old (Dumpy bottle)					80		
Glen Grant – 15-year-old (Triangular decanter)		1600					920
Glen Grant – 15-year-old (G & M, 26 2/3 fl. oz)	34	120	50–55	80	62	30–90	110

Whisky Auction Sale Results (£s)	2000	2001	2002	2003	2004	2005	2006
Glen Grant – Glenlivet – 16-year-old (Cadenhead's, 45.7%)					90		
Glen Grant – 17-year-old (Berry Bros & Rudd)					180		
Glen Grant – Glenlivet – 19-year-old (Cadenhead's)	115						
Glen Grant – 20-year-old – 1976 (First Cask)					34	30–40	50
Glen Grant Directors Reserve – 20-year-old		120	95		105	80	
Glen Grant Directors Reserve – 21-year-old						90–120	
Glen Grant – 21-year-old (G & M)		60		80	50–80		
Glen Grant – 21-year-old (Glass decanter)	100						120
Glen Grant – Glenlivet – 21-year-old – 1957 (Cadenhead's)		80	70				
Glen Grant – 21-year-old – 1961 (Italian import)	70						
Glen Grant – 21-year-old – 1967 (Italian import, decanter)				90			
Glen Grant – 22-year-old – 1961 (Italian import)	60						
Glen Grant – 23-year-old – 1972 (Signatory, 55.8%)				43		75	
Glen Grant – 24-year-old – 1976 (First Cask)					25–45		
Glen Grant – 25-year-old – 1964 (Signatory, 46%)		43			50		
Glen Grant Royal Wedding – 25-year-old	120	140–170	90			90	110–120
Glen Grant – 25-year-old (Silver Jubilee)	125–130	120–130	110–165	100–130	110	130	160
Glen Grant – 25-year-old (G & M)	50–65	55–160		55–62	32–35	30–90	60–75
Glen Grant – 25-year-old (G & M, Securo screw cap)				120			
Glen Grant – 25-year-old (G Strachan)	36	45	120				
Glen Grant – 25-year-old – 1960 (Crystal decanter)		333					
Glen Grant – 26-year-old – 1972 (Hart Bros, 51.1%)		70					
Glen Grant – 27-year-old (G & M, Securo screw cap)				150			
Glen Grant – 27-year-old – 1973 (First Cask)							40
Glen Grant – 29-year-old – 1972 (Hart Bros, 53.6%)					37	45	

Whisky Auction Sale Results (£s)	2000	2001	2002	2003	2004	2005	2006
Glen Grant – 30-year-old (150th Anniversary)	230		170	180	125–160	160–170	140–190
Glen Grant – 30-year-old – 1967 (Signatory, 51.8%)	40						
Glen Grant – 31-year-old – 1965 (First Cask)					70		
Glen Grant – 31-year-old – 1968 (Adelphi, 57.7%)						75	
Glen Grant – 31-year-old – 1969 (Adelphi, 53.9%)							73
Glen Grant – 32-year-old (James Catto)						350	
Glen Grant – 33-year-old – 1969 (Mission Series 2, 46%)							42
Glen Grant – 33-year-old – 1969 (Hart Bros, 51.5%)				40–53	52		35–43
Glen Grant – 33-year-old – 1949 (Crystal decanter)		280				270	
Glen Grant – 33-year-old (G & M)		55		100		45	
Glen Grant – 35-year-old (G & M)	60					90	110
Glen Grant – Glenlivet – 36-year-old – 1964 (Cadenhead's, 52.6%)					90		
Glen Grant – 1974 (SMWS, 62.7%)						190	
Glen Grant – 1979 (SMWS, 50.4%)						50	
Glen Grant – 38-year-old (G & M)	90	60–140		120	90		
Glen Grant – 40-year-old (Crystal decanter)	170						
Glen Grant – 40-year-old (J MacArthur, 48%)	160	120					
Glen Grant – 40-year-old – 1949 (Crystal decanter)	300	250				180	
Glen Grant – 40-year-old – 1959 (47.3%)			260				
Glen Grant – 42-year-old (G & M)	50–155	120	75	130–160	120	105	
Glen Grant – 45-year-old (G & M)	140–155					100–210	270
Glen Grant – 50-year-old – 1936 (G & M)			300				
Glen Grant – 50-year-old – 1948 (G & M, deacanter)					350	200	
Glen Grant – 50-year-old – 1949 (Ian MacLeod & Co., 46%)				1100	500		

Glen Keith

Only a small selection of expressions of Glen Keith have been offered at auction to date

Whisky Auction Sale Results (£s)	2000	2001	2002	2003	2004	2005	2006
Glen Keith – 1965 (G & M)			24–71	23	23–37		
Glen Keith – 1967 (G & M)							55
Glen Keith – 1967 (Italian import)			122				
Glen Keith – 19-year-old – 1963 (G & M)						80–130	
Glen Keith – 20-year-old – 1963 (G & M)							80
Glen Keith – 12-year-old – 1967 (Cadenhead's)	110						
Glen Keith – 30-year-old – 1968 (Old Malt Cask)	45						
Glen Keith – 1973 (SMWS, 58.7%)						115	
Glen Keith – Distilled Pre-1983			23–43	23–50		35	27

Glen Mhor

A varied selection of Glen Mhor has been sold at auction in recent times, early examples are the most popular

Whisky Auction Sale Results (£s)	2000	2001	2002	2003	2004	2005	2006
Glen Mhor Old Highland – Early 20th century		2500					
Glen Mhor – 6-year-old (C MacKinlay & Co, 26 2/3 fl. oz)			200				
Glen Mhor – 8-year-old (C MacKinlay & Co., stopper cork, lead capsule)			800				
Glen Mhor – 8-year-old (G & M)			65–67	70	20–80	27	22–28
Glen Mhor – 10-year-old (Italian import)	110	85	130				
Glen Mhor – 10-year-old (MacKinlay & Birnie)	380–480						
Glen Mhor – 10-year-old (C MacKinlay & Co)				105		290	
Glen Mhor – 10-year-old (C MacKinlay & Co., stopper cork, lead capsule)			800				
Glen Mhor – 14-year-old – 1978 (Signatory, 43%)	35				23		
Glen Mhor – 15-year-old (G & M)					27–33		25–37
Glen Mhor – 15-year-old – 1976 (Cadenhead's, 60.9%)			40		70		
Glen Mhor – 19-year-old – 1976 (Cadenhead's, 57.8%)				47	55		
Glen Mhor – 21-year-old – 1976 (Hart Bros, 43%)		40	28	22	21	30	
Glen Mhor – 1963 (G & M)	65	40		67–80	110	55	
Glen Mhor – 1965 (G & M)	165						
Glen Mhor – 1969 (Campbell & Clark)	70–90	85–110	55–160	80	100	70–90	110–160
Glen Mhor – 1975 (SMWS, 62.1%)		167					
Glen Mhor – 1975 (Cadenhead's, 60.9%)				50			47
Glen Mhor – 1975 (Cadenhead's, 59.1%)					120		

Whisky Auction Sale Results (£s)	2000	2001	2002	2003	2004	2005	2006
Glen Mhor – 1978 (G & M, 65.3%)					33–47		
Glen Mhor – 1978 (G & M, 63.2%)						27	
Glen Mhor – 1978 (G & M, 62.2%)					77		
Glen Mhor – 1979 (G & M, 66.3%)	30				37		
Glen Mhor – 1979 (SMWS, 64.3%)							120
Glen Mhor – 20-year-old – 1977 (Silent Stills)			65				
Glen Mhor – 20-year-old – 1980 (Signatory, 43%)							35
Glen Mhor – 22-year-old – 1979 (61%)							50
Glen Mhor – 25-year-old – 1963 (Crystal decanter)	165						
Glen Mhor – 25-year-old – 1970 (Campbell & Clark)	70–80	80–90			85–100	90	140
Glen Mhor – 26-year-old – 1965 (Signatory, 56.4%)						47–90	
Glen Mhor – 33-year-old – 1966 (Old Malt Cask)						60	
Glen Mhor – 34-year-old – 1966 (Old Malt Cask)		80					
Glen Mhor – 35-year-old – 1966 (Old Malt Cask)						90	
Glen Mhor – 35-year-old (Silent Stills, 49.2%)				115			

Glen Mhor – 15-year-old

Glen Moray

Of the variety of expressions of Glen Moray that have been sold at auction in recent times, mature limited editions and older bottlings have been the most popular

Whisky Auction Sale Results (£s)	2000	2001	2002	2003	2004	2005	2006
Glen Moray Centenary	60–75			60–90	60	65–100	
Glen Moray – Glenlivet – 5-year-old		80					
Glen Moray – Glenlivet – 8-year-old		45					
Glen Moray – 10-year-old (26 2/3 fl. oz)	50		45–50	45	35–53	105	90
Glen Moray – 12-year-old (75 cl.)					20–40	20–27	37
Glen Moray – Glenlivet – 12-year-old – 1992 (Cadenhead's, 61%)					30		
Glen Moray – 15-year-old				65			
Glen Moray – 16-year-old					35		
Glen Moray – 16-year-old (Chenin Blanc)			80				
Glen Moray Vintage – 18-year-old – 1973 (43%)				40			
Glen Moray – 24-year-old – 1962		130	102		120		
Glen Moray – 27-year-old – 1962					90–150	120–160	
Glen Moray – 26-year-old – 1960	97–190		115–145		80–130	60–115	140–190
Glen Moray – 27-year-old – 1964					110–140		
Glen Moray – 28-year-old – 1971						75–100	
Glen Moray – 25-year-old – 1965 (ANA Airways)					160		
Glen Moray – 26-year-old – 1966	97–120			80	90–160		170
Glen Moray Vintage – 1959 (50.9%)					320	340	
Glen Moray Vintage – 1966		150					
Glen Moray Vintage – 1971					90		

Whisky Auction Sale Results (£s)	2000	2001	2002	2003	2004	2005	2006
Glen Moray Distillery Managers Choice – 1974 (53.4%)					48		80
Glen Moray Vintage – 1981 (57.7%)			67		75	70	80
Glen Moray – 27-year-old – 1959 (Cadenhead's)	45						
Glen Moray – 30-year-old – 1959 (R W Duthie, 44.1%)		400			200		
Glen Moray – 30-year-old – 1959 (Signatory)			130				
Glen Moray – Glenlivet – 30-year-old (Cadenhead's, 48.8%)					90–110		

Glen Moray – 26-year-old – 1960

Glen Scotia

Few examples of Glen Scotia have been seen at auction in recent times, older bottlings are quite popular

Whisky Auction Sale Results (£s)	2000	2001	2002	2003	2004	2005	2006
Glen Scotia – 5-year-old (Gillies & Co)		70	77–85				90
Glen Scotia – 8-year-old (Gilles & Co)		65		45	25–40	37–40	
Glen Scotia – 14-year-old (70 cl.)			35		20		
Glen Scotia – 12-year-old (Ceramic decanter)		65					
Glen Scotia – 12-year-old (Gillies & Co., 54%)	70	55–90					
Glen Scotia – 1973	50						
Glen Scotia – 13-year-old – 1977 (Cadenhead's)	60						
Glen Scotia – 27-year-old – 1966 (Signatory, 51.5%)			140	50			
Glen Scotia – 28-year-old – 1975 (46%)						55	42

Glenallachie

The example below is the only distillery bottling that has appeared at auction in recent times with only a few independent bottlings appearing

Whisky Auction Sale Results (£s)	2000	2001	2002	2003	2004	2005	2006
Glenallachie – Glenlivet – 12-year-old (75 cl.)		350	75		52–70		60
Glenallachie – 1969 (G & M, 56.8%)		37					
Glenallachie – Glenlivet – 12-year-old – 1970 (75 cl.)			50			30–130	
Glenallachie – 18-year-old – 1976 (Castle Collection, 43%)					38		
Glenallachie – 11-year-old – 1985 (Signatory, 43%)			27	18			
Glenallachie – 31-year-old – 1971 (Douglas Laing, 53.8%)						80	

Glenallachie – Glenlivet – 12-year-old

Glenburgie

A variety of expressions of Glenburgie have come up at auction recently

Whisky Auction Sale Results (£s)	2000	2001	2002	2003	2004	2005	2006
Glenburgie (Royal Wedding)					65	80–95	
Glenburgie – 5-year-old (75 cl.)				60			
Glenburgie – 8-year-old (G & M, 70 cl.)					20		
Glenburgie – 15-year-old (Allied Distillers)				32	20–30	18–27	
Glenburgie – 15-year-old – 1968 (G & M)	58				70	100	70
Genburgie – Glenlivet – 16-year-old – 1962 (Cadenhead's, 45.7%)					90–110		
Glenburgie – 1948 (G & M Centenary Reserve)		200			230	90	
Glenburgie – 1961 (G & M, 40%)						65	
Glenburgie – 1966 (G & M, 61.2%)					33–47		
Glenburgie – 1966 (G & M, 57.7%)					65		
Glenburgie – 1968 (G & M)				30–35	27–32		
Glenburgie – 18-year-old (J & G Stoddart, 70 cl.)			50	35			
Glenburgie – 22-year-old – 1975 (Signatory, 56.6%)	40						
Glenburgie – 30-year-old – 1954 (G & M)				150			
Glenburgie – 30-year-old – 1954 (G & M, crystal decanter)		333					
Glenburgie – 32-year-old – 1968 (Hart Bros, 52.6%)				35	38		
Glenburgie – 33-year-old – 1949 (G & M)				140			
Glenburgie – 33-year-old – 1967 (Signatory, 53%)						60	
Glenburgie – 35-year-old – 1966 (Hart Bros, 40.5%)						37	60

Whisky Auction Sale Results (£s)	2000	2001	2002	2003	2004	2005	2006
Glenburgie – 37-year-old – 1962 (Italian import, 45%)	150	120					
Glenburgie – Glenlivet – 37-year-old 1962 (Signatory, 51.1%)					90		

Glencadam

Very few expressions of Glencadam have appeared at auction so far, the rarest being a 6-year-old

Whisky Auction Sale Results (£s)	2000	2001	2002	2003	2004	2005	2006
Glencadam – 6-year-old (A J Thomson & Co)	520					300	
Glencadam – 25-year-old (Crystal decanter)		250	200				
Glencadam – 12-year-old – 1974 (G & M)						100	
Glencadam – 14-year-old – 1964 (Cadenhead's)			110		80	72	140
Glencadam – 15-year-old – 1967 (G & M)						70	
Glencadam – 18-year-old – 1965 (G & M)				60			
Glencadam – 15-year-old – 1980 (Signatory, 43%)			37				
Glencadam – 15-year-old (Allied Distillers)				32	17–30	18–27	
Glencadam – 29-year-old – 1972 (First Cask , 46%)					60		
Glencadam – 1973 (SMWS, 57.3%)		167					
Glencadam – 1974 (G & M)	28–46		22–32	21–35	40	20–38	
Glencadam – 1987 (G & M)						24	

Glencadam – 14-year-old
(Cadenhead's)

Glendronach

Some fine examples of The Glendronach come up at auction, this malt is really quite sought after

Whisky Auction Sale Results (£s)	2000	2001	2002	2003	2004	2005	2006
Glendronach – Circa 1930	700			480			
Glendronach – 150th Anniversary (1826–1976)				800	620–700		
Glendronach – 8-year-old (Tall green 26 2/3 fl. oz)		70	53–82		40–75	45–90	
Glendronach – 8-year-old (Discoloured label)	25						
Glendronach – 12-year-old (75 cl.)	36	50	73–87	53	40–70	35–55	57–77
Glendronach – 12-year-old – 1962			90				
Glendronach – 12-year-old (Dumpy green bottle, 75 cl.)	65		53–65	37	67–75		77–80
Glendronach Original – 12-year-old (75 cl.)	28–36	30–50	41–65	27–33			37
Glendronach Traditional – 12-year-old	28	35			45–62		

Left to right.
Glendronach – Circa 1930,
Glendronach – 150th Anniversary

Whisky Auction Sale Results (£s)	2000	2001	2002	2003	2004	2005	2006
Glendronach – 12-year-old – 1962	65						
Glendronach – 12-year-old – 1963						95–105	
Glendronach – 15-year-old (40%)					45		80
Glendronach – 1970 (Signatory)	310						
Glendronach – 1970 (R W Duthie)		130					
Glendronach – 1971 (SMWS, 54.9%)			147				
Glendronach The Millennium Malt – 1972 (48%)	45	150					120
Glendronach – 18-year-old – 1972			33		50–57		
Glendronach – 18-year-old – 1975	36	50		53	57		
Glendronach – 18-year-old – 1976	28					70	
Glendronach – 18-year-old – 1977			35				
Glendronach – 19-year-old (US export, 45%)		450			400		
Glendronach – 20-year-old – 1970 (Signatory, Sailing Ships, 43%)		80		50–100			
Glendronach – 20-year-old – 1970 (Dun Eideann, 43%)					80		
Glendronach – 23-year-old – 1955 (G & M)			170	160			
Glendronach – 23-year-old – 1975 (First Cask, 46%)					40	30	
Glendronach – 27-year-old – 1955 (G & M)				150			
Glendronach – 25-year-old (Signatory, 41.2%)					45		
Glendronach – 25-year-old – 1968 (Nippon Airways)		250	200	110	150		120–130
Glendronach – 25-year-old – 1968		100–105			65		65
Glendronach – 27-year-old – 1972 (Inc. of Maltmen, 48%)				90			140
Glendronach – 27-year-old – 1976 (Mission Series 4, 46%)							40
Glendronach – 33-year-old – (40%)							160

Glendullan

The Glendullan Manager's Dram has held it's value steadily over recent years and early distillery bottlings are very popular too

Whisky Auction Sale Results (£s)	2000	2001	2002	2003	2004	2005	2006
Glendullan – 11-year-old – 1981 (Signatory, 40%)						27	
Glendullan – 12-year-old (MacDonald Greenlees, 26 2/3 fl. oz)			75–120	70–135	50–90	47–135	75
Glendullan – 12-year-old (Flora & Fauna)	38		30–33	26			33–50
Glendullan Centenary – 16-year-old (65.9%)	95–140	100–140	85	80–90	60–150	60–90	
Glendullan Centenary – 16-year-old (Classic Malts, 62.6%)				35	40–60		
Glendullan – 18-year-old (Manager's Dram)	175–193	140–160	160–250	110–160	130–200	100–170	
Glendullan – 22-year-old – 1972 (62.6%)		43			37–65		
Glendullan – 23-year-old – 1972 (62.43%)	28		55–83	40	32	63	160
Glendullan – 23-year-old – 1973 (58.6%)	36	53	36–80		90		
Glendullan – 23-year-old – 1974 (63.1%)				35	32		60
Glendullan – 1979 (SMWS, 67.8%)						60	
Glendullan – Glenlivet – 32 year-old – 1967 (Cadenhead's, 48.1%)						65	
Glendullan – 36-year-old – 1966 (Douglas Laing, 55.1%)						95	70

Glenfarclas

Some fine examples of Glenfarclas come up at auction, older expressions attract great interest, as do the wide and varied range of bottlings spanning many years

Whisky Auction Sale Results (£s)	2000	2001	2002	2003	2004	2005	2006
Glenfarclas – Glenlivet – Believed Early 20th century (J G Thomson & Co)		2100					
Glenfarclas – 8-year-old – Early 20th century (J G Thomson & Co)	650					110	
Glenfarclas 150th Anniversary	105–140		120–130	90–120	90–140	150	160–190
Glenfarclas – 1836–1986 (150th Anniversary)		520					
Glenfarclas – 1836–1986 (150th Anniversary, boxed with four glasses)		600				520	
Glenfarclas 1124 Society of St. Giles'							210
Glenfarclas 105 – 8-year-old	32		50	50			
Glenfarclas – 5-year-old (Grant Bonding Co)		80					
Glenfarclas – 7-year-old (Grant Bonding Co)	85						
Glenfarclas – 8-year-old (Grant Bonding Co)	120–133		95		110		
Glenfarclas – Glenlivet – 8-year-old (Grant Bonding Co)			50–85		125	210–300	200–290
Glenfarclas – 8-year-old (Italian import)	85						
Glenfarclas – 8-year-old (Saccone & Speed)	43				88		60
Round Table Reserve – Over 8-year-old (J & G Grant International)		270					
Glenfarclas – 10-year-old (Italian import)	43						
Glenfarclas – 10-year-old (75 cl.)							37
Glenfarclas – 12-year-old	50						

Whisky Auction Sale Results (£s)	2000	2001	2002	2003	2004	2005	2006
Glenfarclas – 12-year-old (Donside Paper Centenary)					110		
Glenfarclas – 15-year-old	32						37
Glenfarclas Silk Cut – 15-year-old							190
Glenfarclas – Glenlivet – 15-year-old (Grant Bonding Co)				100			
Glenfarclas – 15-year-old (Dumpy square bottle, 80 proof)	50			100	40–67		
Glenfarclas – 17-year-old	43						
Royal Findhorn Yacht Club – 20-year-old		90					

Left to right. Glenfarclas – 150th Anniversary, Glenfarclas – 1961, Glenfarclas – Glenlivet – 8-year-old

Whisky Auction Sale Results (£s)	2000	2001	2002	2003	2004	2005	2006
Glenfarclas – 20-year-old – 1969 (Signatory, 58.2%)	330						
Glenfarclas – 21-year-old (Grant Bonding Co, dumpy)	32–43					52–70	60
Glenfarclas – 22-year-old (Millennium)		40	35–45	58	55	50	45
Glenfarclas – 25-year-old (Grant Bonding Co, dumpy)	32–43			100	50–60		
Glenfarclas – 25-year-old (Jim Clark commemorative)			130				
Glenfarclas – 30-year-old			77		55–65		
Glenfarclas – 30-year-old – 1964 (Signatory, 54.1%)		90			100		
Glenfarclas – 31-year-old (Cadenhead's, 54.4%)					45		
Glenfarclas – 40-year-old – 1958 (Signatory glass decanter, 52.8%)		340	390			300	230
Glenfarclas – 40-year-old (Millennium)				720	760		
Glenfarclas – 1954 (43%)						180	
Glenfarclas – 1955 (Private bottling, 43%)		320					
Glenfarclas Christmas, 1959 (46%)							480
Glenfarclas – 1961 (Oval crystal decanter)		420					700
Glenfarclas – 1961 (Wooden case)	220	170			240		300–310
Glenfarclas – 1961 (Lacking case)	140						
Glenfarclas – 1966 (German export, 46%)	180						
Glenfarclas Vintage – 1966 (46%)		120					130
Glenfarclas – 1966 (51.2%)						130	240
Glenfarclas – 1967 (57.3%)		120					
Glenfarclas – 1967 (stone jar, 57.3%)		120					
Glenfarclas – 1968 (stone jar, 52.1%)		110					
Glenfarclas – 1968 (stone jar, 54.2%)		115					
Glenfarclas – 1968		95	75	45–50			

Whisky Auction Sale Results (&s)	2000	2001	2002	2003	2004	2005	2006
Glenfarclas – 1969 (54%)							310
Glenfarclas – 1970 (52.3%)							160
Glenfarclas – 1970 (stone jar)		130					
Glenfarclas A Dusky Maiden (SMWS, 53.5)					90		
Glenfarclas – 1972 (German export)		56				37	
Glenfarclas – 1972 (Craigellachie Hotel, 51.2%)				130			
Glenfarclas – 1973 (SMWS, 51.5%)		189					
Glenfarclas Vintage – 1973		65					
Glenfarclas – 1974					80		
Glenfarclas – 1975 (43%)							200
Glenfarclas – 1975 (SMWS, 55.5%)							90
Glenfarclas – 1976 (43%)							100
Glenfarclas – 1976 (52.6%)							120
Glenfarclas – 1977		55–56					
Glenfarclas – 1978 (SMWS, 54.7%)					55		
Glenfarclas Vintage – 1978 (43%)		45–65	47				
Glenfarclas Vintage – 1978 (53.5%)			47				145
Glenfarclas – 1978 (51.7%)							145
Glenfarclas – 1978 (54.3%)							145
Glenfarclas – 1978 (45.5%)							145
Glenfarclas – 1979		65					
Glenfarclas Vintage – 1987						37	
Glenfarclas – 1990 (Family Malt Collection)						37	

Glenfiddich

Early examples of Glenfiddich make a rare appearance at auction, the wide and varied range of bottlings spanning a variety of years illustrate the various expressions available

Whisky Auction Sale Results (£s)	2000	2001	2002	2003	2004	2005	2006
Glenfiddich – Early 20th century	1350–1400	2100					
Glenfiddich – Early 20th century (Poor condition)			480				
Glenfiddich – Circa 1930	1600						
Glenfiddich Highland Crock					27–60	30	35–37
Glenfiddich Centenary	80–145	65–85	60–100	95–115	90–130	120–150	120–140
Glenfiddich (ADRA Equine Fund, 1991)			80				
Glenfiddich Straight Malt					170		180
Glenfiddich Straight Malt – 8-year-old		300–320				420	310–700
Glenfiddich – Over 8-year-old			60–87	55–97	52	90	40–85
Glenfiddich Solera Reserve – 15-year-old						20–23	
Glenfiidich – Cask Strength – 15-year-old (51%)						22–23	
Glenfiddich – Glenlivet – 17-year-old (Cadenhead's, 46%)					36–45		
Glenfiddich – 16-year-old – 1979 (Italian import, 46%)		190					
Glenfiddich – 18-year-old (Spode decanter)	25–48	35			35–60		
Glenfiddich Ancient Reserve – 18-year-old				27	35		53–55
Glenfiddich Superior Reserve – 18-year-old	40	60					53–90
Glenfiddich Excellence – 18-year-old	30	80			40		30–70
Glenfiddich Excellence – 18-year-old (With gilt & marble plinth)				270			
Glenfiddich Millennium Reserve – 21-year-old					50		

RoyalMilewhiskies

www.royalmilewhiskies.com

379 HIGH STREET, THE ROYAL MILE, EDINBURGH
3 BLOOMSBURY STREET, (Nr BRITISH MUSEUM), LONDON

Whisky Auction Sale Results (£s)	2000	2001	2002	2003	2004	2005	2006
Glenfiddich Gran Reserva – 21-year-old					65–80		
Glenfiddich – 21-year-old (Wedgwood decanter)	85–110	80		80		150	95
Glenfiddich – 24-year-old – 1977 (40%)							360
Glenfiddich – 1936 (P J Russell & Co, 45%)	780						
Glenfiddich – 1952 (Re-opening of Reception Centre, 1969, 75 degrees)				700			
Glenfiddich – 21-year-old – 1957 (Cadenhead's)	170						
Glenfiddich – 21-year-old – 1961 (Italian import, 45%)	75	145					
Glenfiddich – 22-year-old – 1961 (Nadi Fiori, 45%)	360						
Glenfiddich – Glenlivet – 23-year-old – 1973 (Cadenhead's, 47.8%)						50	
Glenfiddich – 1964 (J & J Hunter, Belfast, 58%)			170	200	210	200	
Glenfiddich – Glenlivet – 30-year-old – 1963 (Cadenhead's, 51.7%)					120		
Glenfiddich – 30-year-old					70		
Glenfiddich –Glenlivet – 31-year-old – 1973 (Cadenhead's, 48.9%)							70
Glenfiddich – 37-year-old – 1964 (I Macleod & Co, 58.7%)			300	140–150			
Glenfiddich Vintage Reserve – 25-year-old – 1973 (Cask 11148, 49.2%)		240					
Glenfiddich – 29-year-old – 1956 (Italian import, 50.6%)	210	360					
Glenfiddich – 30-year-old (Stag's head silver & crystal decanter)				1300			
Glenfiddich Stag's Head Decanter (Lacking contents)					140		

Whisky Auction Sale Results (£s)	2000	2001	2002	2003	2004	2005	2006
Glenfiddich Vintage Reserve – 30-year-old – 1967 (Cask 3959, 43.6%)			330		160		
Glenfiddich Vintage Reserve – 30-year-old – 1968 (Cask 13142, 49.2%)				160			
Glenfiddich Vintage Reserve – 30-year-old – 1973 (Cask 7571, 49.8%)						150	
Glenfiddich – Glenlivet – 31-year-old – 1973 (Cadenhead's, 48.9%)						90	
Glenfiddich – Glenlivet – 31-year-old – 1973 (Cadenhead's, 46.9%)						90	
Glenfiddich Private Vintage – 1975 (55.7%)							180
Glenfiddich Vintage Reserve – 35-year-old – 1961 (Cask 9015, 43.2%)			340		290		
Glenfiddich Vintage Reserve – 35-year-old – 1963 (Cask 12371, 47.6%)	210–290		210				

Left to right.
Glenfiddich Excellence – 18-year-old,
Glenfiddich Classic, Glenfiddich – Over 8-year-old,
Glenfiddich Straight Malt – 8-year-old

Whisky Auction Sale Results (£s)	2000	2001	2002	2003	2004	2005	2006
Glenfiddich – Glenlivet – 35-year-old – 1965 (Cadenhead's, 49.1%)					110		
Glenfiddich – Glenlivet – 35-year-old – 1967 (Cadenhead's, 42.4%)					170		
Glenfiddich Vintage Reserve – Over 40-year-old – 1959 (Bottle No 3 of 6)	2100						
Glenfiddich Rare Collection – Over 40-year-old (43.6%)			1500		550		650–700
Glenfiddich – 40-year-old – 1964 (Hart Bros, 47.5%)						270	280
Glenfiddich – 50-year-old		4300		3200			
Glenfiddich – 50-year-old (Miniature ceramic decanter)				400			
Glenfiddich Millennium Reserve – 1984 (40%)						42	

Left to right. Glenfiddich – Early 20th Century, Glenfiddich Straight Malt, Glenfiddich – 1952, Glenfiddich Rare Collection

Glenflagler

Older expressions of Glenflagler are now quite rare, the cask strength Signatory bottlings have achieved healthy prices at auction in addition to early distillery bottlings

Whisky Auction Sale Results (£s)	2000	2001	2002	2003	2004	2005	2006
Glenflagler (26 2/3 fl. ozs)	130					130–140	230
Glenflagler – 5-year-old (75 cl.)			170			100–130	130–170
Glenflagler – 8-year-old (70 cl.)	70	80					
Glenflagler – 8-year-old (26 2/3 fl. ozs)		250	160		210		260
Glenflagler – 8-year-old (Austrian import)		230					
Glenflagler – 12-year-old (Inver House, 75cl.)	65				115		
Glenflagler – 12-year-old (Spanish import)		110					
Glenflagler – 23-year-old – 1970 (Signatory, 50.1%)	170–225	190			110	165	
Glenflagler – 23-year-old – 1970 (Signatory, 50.1%, miniature)			107			55	
Glenflagler – 1973 (46%)						270	
Glenflagler – 23-year-old – 1972 (Signatory, 51.3%)	155	185–200	190		140–155	220	170
Glenflagler – 23-year-old – 1972 (Signatory, 50.1%)	300				150		
Glenflagler – 24-year-old – 1972 (Signatory, 52%)		210					

Glengarioch

There have only been a few examples of Glengarioch sold at auction recently, the rarest being the Bicentenary bottling

Whisky Auction Sale Results (£s)	2000	2001	2002	2003	2004	2005	2006
Glen Garioch (26 2/3 fl. oz)			55–75		62		
Glengarioch – Over 8-year-old (26 2/3 fl. oz)		80		100	130		
Glen Garioch – 10-year-old (75cl)		60					57
Glen Garioch – 15-year-old (Bi-centenary)				240	300	400	
Glen Garioch – 16-year-old – 1986 (54.4%)							47
Glen Garioch – 18-year-old – 1978 (59.4%)			45				50
Glengarioch – 20-year-old – 1957 (Cadenhead's, 80 degrees proof)				120			
Glengarioch – 21-year-old (43%)	40–55				45–65		30–65
Glengarioch – 21-year-old (Italian import, 50%)		130–225					
Glengarioch – 21-year-old – 1965 (43%)	45–65	55	45–90	90	34	90–95	
Glengarioch – 27-year-old – 1970 (49.6%)	130						140
Glengarioch – 29-year-old – 1968 (56.6%)	70			45		130	
Glengarioch – 29-year-old – 1968 (56.3%)				100			140
Glengarioch – 1971 (Italian import, 59.6%)	90–150						
Glen Garioch – 1971 (43%)			70				
Glen Garioch – 1971 (59.6%)			150	150			
Glen Garioch – 1976 (SMWS, 60.4%)							70
Glen Garioch – 1984 (40%)						47	
Glen Garioch – 1987 (40%)					70		40

Glenglassaugh

A variety of examples of Glenglassaugh have appeared at auction in recent years

Whisky Auction Sale Results (£s)	2000	2001	2002	2003	2004	2005	2006
Glenglassaugh – 12-year-old			75	30	30–40	62	30
Glenglassaugh – 1964 (SMWS, 46.8%)						110–155	
Glenglassaugh – 1967 (G & M)	60				37		
Glenglassaugh – 17-year-old – 1967 (G & M)						80–90	
Glenglassaugh – 1967 (SMWS, 52.6%)					100		
Glenglassaugh Family Silver – 1973			30		33–50	62	55–65
Glenglassaugh – 1983 (G & M)	46	38	26–40		33–42		
Glenglassaugh – 1986 (G & M)					26		
Glenglassaugh – 22-year-old – 1974 (Hart Bros, 43%))				30		37	
Glenglassaugh – 22-year-old – 1978 (Cadenhead's, 48.8%)					55		
Glenglassaugh – 31-year-old – 1967 (Silent Stills)	52	100					

Glenglassaugh The Family Silver – 1968

Glengoyne

Of the variety of expressions of Glengoyne a rare distillery bottling, The Middlecut and Farewell Dram have achieved the best prices at auction to date

Whisky Auction Sale Results (£s)	2000	2001	2002	2003	2004	2005	2006
Glengoyne Single Cask (56.2%)				60			
Glengoyne Scottish Oak (53.5%)						33	45–47
Glengoyne – 8-year-old (26 2/3 fl. oz)			45–82	55–80	50	62–115	80
Glengoyne – 8-year-old (Italian import)		50					
Glengoyne – Guaranteed over 10-year-old					1150		
Glengoyne – 10-year-old (75 cl.)		30		55	55	23–62	90
Glengoyne – 12-year-old		50					
Glengoyne Kiln Decanter – 15-year-old		90–260	170		100		
Glengoyne Kiln Decanter – 15-year-old (Condition poor)		75					
Glengoyne – 17-year-old	21	16–30			26	30–42	
Glengoyne – 21-year-old		30	47		28	52	
Glengoyne Vintage Reserve – 25-year-old – 1968 (50.3%)			30–80	33–70	60–80	85	
Glengoyne – 28-year-old (50.4%)						180	
Glengoyne – 30-year-old (43%)							100
Glengoyne – 30-year-old (Millennium clock)			320		320	240–250	
Glengoyne 2000 AD – 30-year-old (51.3%)							200
Glengoyne – 1967 (47.7%)	40						
Glengoyne The Middle Cut – 1967 (52.5%)	660			420			
Glengoyne Vintage Reserve – 1967	65	75–140		70–90	60–100		65–100
Glengoyne Winter Distillation – 1967 (47.7%)						100	

Whisky Auction Sale Results (£s)	2000	2001	2002	2003	2004	2005	2006
Glengoyne Single Cask – 1968 (51.7%)				90			
Glengoyne Vintage Reserve – 1968		70	47–80		75–90	80	50–95
Glengoyne J E – 27-year-old – 1969 (52.5%)					270	230–360	
Glengoyne – 28-year-old (50.4%)							140
Glengoyne Vintage Reserve – 1969 (47%)	80	135	80		80	90–110	70–180
Glengoyne Single Cask – 1969 (54.4%)				60			
Glengoyne Farewell Dram – 1969 (54.4%)	350	400				300	
Glengoyne Single Cask – 1970 (56%)				50			70
Glengoyne Single Cask – 1970 (53.4%)				50			
Glengoyne Single Cask – 1970 (51.5%)						52	
Glengoyne Vintage Reserve – 1970 (48.5%)			80	50–70	80	100	60
Glengoyne Single Cask – 1971 (56.2%)				52			
Glengoyne Vintage Reserve – 1971			47–80				
Glengoyne Vintage – 1971 (48.5%)		90		52			
Glengoyne Vintage Reserve – 1972			80				
Glengoyne Single Cask – 1972 (55.9%)		100		57		110	
Glengoyne Single Cask – 1972 (56%)							80
Glengoyne – Vintage 1972 (57.8%)	85						
Glengoyne Single Cask – 1984 (54.4%)							38
Glengoyne Single Cask – 1985 (59.1%)		70					85

Glenlivet

The Glenlivet Special Export Reserve – 34-year-old has performed well at auction, the many bottlings spanning a variety of years show the huge range of expressions available

Whisky Auction Sale Results (£s)	2000	2001	2002	2003	2004	2005	2006
Glenlivet – 1888 (W M Nicholls, Glasgow)		2300					
Glenlivet Special Reserve – 9-year-old – 1900 (J G Thomson & Co)	1500						
Old Glenlivet Whisky – Believed late 19th century (MacLean & Son, Edinburgh, magnum)						400	
Glenlivet Liqueur – Believed circa 1940 (Mayor Sworder & Co)	130	105–150					
Glenlivet, Old Blended (W Lumsden, Aberdeen)		110–170	120–135				
Glenlivet Special Export Reserve (no age)		90					
Glenlivet (Cadenhead's, 70 degrees proof)				180			
Glenlivet – Over 7-year-old (Campbell, Hope & King)	360						150
Glenlivet K – 8-year-old (Hatch Mansfield)						100–120	80–115
Glenlivet – 8-year-old (G & M, 26 2/3 fl. oz)			47–80		60	50–90	55
Glenlivet – 10-year-old – 1971 (W Glennie, 40%)						220	
Glenlivet – 12-year-old (26 2/3 fl. oz)			60–110				60–160
Glenlivet – 12-year-old (45.7%)		175					
Glenlivet – 12-year-old (75 cl., 70 degrees proof)					30–55	43–52	
Glenlivet – 12-year-old – 1964 (Peter Dominic)		280		350			
Glenlivet – 12-year-old – 1965 (Peter Dominic)		260					90
Glenlivet – 12-year-old – 1969 (Peter Dominic)							240

Whisky Auction Sale Results (£s)	2000	2001	2002	2003	2004	2005	2006
Glenlivet – 14-year-old – 1964 (Cadenhead's, 45.7%)						120	
Glenlivet – 15-year-old (G & M)		75		80	40–75	75–90	70–75
Glenlivet – 15-year-old (G & M, cask strength))	83	80	40	75			
Glenlivet – 18-year-old – 1951		175					
Glenlivet – 20-year-old (Italian export, 45.7%)						170	
Glenlivet – 21-year-old		130	170				
Glenlivet – 21-year-old (G & M)		45				65	35
Glenlivet – 21-year-old (Crystal decanter)						220	
Glenlivet – 21-year-old (In leather suitcase)	300	290				230	

Left to right.
Old Blended Glenlivet,
The Glenlivet (Cadenhead's)

Whisky Auction Sale Results (£s)	2000	2001	2002	2003	2004	2005	2006
Glenlivet Archive – 21-year-old							40
Glenlivet Highland Lady – 21-year-old						65	
Glenlivet Ashworth OBE – 22 years service						310	
Glenlivet – 21-year-old – 1957 (Cadenhead's)		75					
Glenlivet – 21-year-old – 1963 (Chairman's Reserve)		460	310–400				380–420
Glenlivet – 21-year-old – 1963 (G & M, 75 cl.)			70–90	75–80			
Glenlivet Liqueur – over 22-year-old (J Leslie, Fort Augustus)		1150					
Glenlivet – 1974 (Malt Master, 43%)						40–67	
Glenlivet – 20-year-old – 1975 (First Cask, 46%)					40		
Glenlivet – 21-year-old – 1973 (First Cask, 46%)					34		
Glenlivet – 22-year-old – 1974 (Hart Bros, 43%)						37	
Glenlivet – 23-year-old – 1974 (Hart Bros, 43%)			25			37	32–35
Glenlivet – 24-year-old – 1974 (First Cask, 46%)					70	40	
Glenlivet – 24-year-old – 1976 (First Cask, 46%)					25–45	35	40
Glenlivet – 25-year-old – 1973 (Whisky Connoisseur, 54.2%)						50	
Glenlivet – 25-year-old (G & M Silver Jubilee)	115						
Glenlivet Wedding Reserve – 25-year-old	150	200–240	230–300	240	240–430	160–310	310–360
Glenlivet Jubilee Reserve – 25-year-old	95–300	230–290	180–270		230–450	200–380	230–410
Glenlivet – 27-year-old – 1968 (First Cask)			38				
Glenlivet – 27-year-old – 1954 (Cadenhead's, 46%)							280
Glenlivet – 28-year-old – 1968 (First Cask)		43					
Glenlivet – 28-year-old – 1974 (Mission, Ser. 1, 46%)							40

Whisky Auction Sale Results (£s)	2000	2001	2002	2003	2004	2005	2006
Glenlivet – 30-year-old – 1972 (Cooper's Choice, 46%)							33
Glenlivet – 31-year-old – 1974 (Mission, Ser. 1, 46%)							38
Glenlivet – 32-year-old – 1968 (Hart Bros)		60–70					
Glenlivet – 32-year-old – 1971 (Cooper's Choice, 46%)						43–45	33
Glenlivet – 33-year-old – 1969 (Douglas Laing, 57.4%)						90	70
Glenlivet – 34-year-old – 1968 (Hart Bros, 50.6%)					50	30–37	
Glenlivet – 34-year-old – 1968 (Peerless Collection, 45.9%)					75		
Glenlivet Special Export Reserve – 34-year-old	400–580	500	440		560	650	580
Glenlivet Special Export Reserve – 34-year-old (Poor labelling)					250–310		
Glenlivet – 36-year-old – 1968 (Celtic Heartlands, 41.2%)							160
Glenlivet – 1937 (G & M, Securo screw cap, 26 2/3 fl. oz)				350		350	
Glenlivet – 1938 (G & M)	155–200	180–270	220	360	205–215	210	190–420
Glenlivet – 1939 (G & M)		150	130	240–270			
Glenlivet – 1940 (G & M)	110	260	310	130			
Glenlivet – 1943 (G & M)		280–340			220		220
Glenlivet – 55-year-old – 1943 (G & M)						650	
Glenlivet – 1946 (G & M)		200				250	140
Glenlivet – 40-year-old – 1946 (G & M)		350					
Glenlivet – 40-year-old – 1948 (G & M, decanter)	220–310	340					
Glenlivet – 42-year-old – 1940 (G & M, decanter)		333					
Glenlivet – 45-year-old – 1940 (G & M)	145	280					

| --- | --- | --- | --- | --- | --- | --- | --- |
Glenlivet – 45-year-old – 1940 (G & M, decanter)		300					
Glenlivet – 49-year-old – 1938 (Sestante jug)	410						
Glenlivet – 49-year-old – 1940 (G & M, decanter)	320						
Glenlivet – 50-year-old – 1940 (G & M, decanter)	250					200–320	
Glenlivet – 1946 (Berry Bros & Rudd)		360					
Glenlivet – 1949 (G & M)							180
Glenlivet – 1956 (G & M)		140–170			105		
Glenlivet – 1959 (75 cl., 43%)					400		
Glenlivet Cellar Collection – 1959 (42.19%)						320	
Glenlivet – 1961 (G & M, 75 cl.)					105		80
Glenlivet – 1961 (Wooden case, 43%)							400
Glenlvet – 1965 (G & M)							60
Glenlivet Vintages – 1967–72 (5 x 20 cl.)		90			130–160	160–210	170
Glenlivet Cellar Collection – 1967 (46%)			170–200	130	210	150–220	150–200
Glenlivet Vintage – 1969 (52.76%)	90					120	
Glenlivet – 1971 (SMWS)						40	
Glenlivet Vintage – 1972			120				
Glenlivet – 1972 (Cooper's Choice, 46%)				50–55	50–55		
Glenlivet – 1972 (SMWS 5th Anniversary, 57.9%)							110
Glenlivet – 1974 (SMWS, 57.4%)		50					
Glenlivet – 1974 (McDowall, 43%)							40
Glenlivet – 1976 (SMWS, 59.6%)		60					
Glenlivet French Oak Finish – 1983 (46%)						50	60

Glenlochy

These examples of Glenlochy listed are the only ones that have appeared at auction in recent years, the mature cask strength examples attract the most interest

Whisky Auction Sale Results (£s)	2000	2001	2002	2003	2004	2005	2006
Glenlochy – 1974 (G & M)			25–71	21–27	25–43	30	
Glenlochy – 13-year-old – 1974 (G & M)						80	60
Glenlochy – 1977 (G & M)	28–46			43–47	40	30	30
Glenlochy – 1977 (Cadenhead's, 41.5%)					30–42		
Glenlochy – 14-year-old – 1968 (G & M)					110	80–100	
Glenlochy – 15-year-old – 1968 (G & M)					80	80	
Glen Lochy – 20-year-old – 1967 (Cadenhead's, 46%)						110	
Glenlochy – 21-year-old – 1977 (Cadenhead's, 57.4%)						60	
Glenlochy – 22-year-old – 1977 (Cadenhead's, 41.5%)				85	80		
Glenlochy – 26-year-old – 1969 (58.8%)	36	28–107	53–83	200	100–140	90–200	210
Glenlochy – 27-year-old – 1974 (Signatory, 53.5%)							70
Glenlochy – 32-year-old – 1963 (Signatory, 51.6%)		100					
Glenlochy – 32-year-old – 1965 (Signatory, Silent Stills, 47.9%)					110	100	
Glenlochy – 49-year-old – 1952 (Old Malt Cask, 43%)		420	180	110		190–300	

Glenlossie

These examples of Glenlossie that have been sold at auction in recent times are mainly independent bottlings

Whisky Auction Sale Results (£s)	2000	2001	2002	2003	2004	2005	2006
Glenlossie – 10-year-old (Flora & Fauna)			27		32–40		25–50
Glenlossie – 43-year-old – 1938 (G & M)		250		150			240
Glenlossie – 1961 (G & M)					50		
Glenlossie – 12-year-old (Manager's Dram)						110–130	
Glenlossie – 14-year-old – 1968 (G & M)	57			60			
Glenlossie – 16-year-old (Crystal decanter)	165–300	250					
Glenlossie – 17-year-old – 1968 (G & M)					55	80	
Glenlossie – 17-year-old – 1981 (Adelphi, 59%)							22
Glenlossie – 19-year-old – 1978 (Hart Bros)				22			
Glenlossie – 1971 (G & M)		50			27–40		
Glenlossie – 1972 (G & M)					40		
Glenlossie – 1974 (G & M)							32
Glenlossie – 1975 (SMWS, 58.5%)		167				105	
Glenlossie – 1975 (SMWS, 46.1%)						110	
Glenlossie – 21-year-old – 1957 (Cadenhead's)	100	75	80				170
Glenlossie – 24-year-old – 1975 (Cadenhead's, 53.9%)		150			80		
Glenlossie – 27-year-old – 1975 (Mission Series 2, 46%)							42

Glenmorangie

Glenmorangie – 1963 has seen tremendous growth at auction over the last 20 years, the expressions of the brand show the diverse range of bottlings available many of which are now very rare

Whisky Auction Sale Results (£s)	2000	2001	2002	2003	2004	2005	2006
Glenmorangie Special Reserve (Distilled 1980–90)			30	22	27	25	
Glenmorangie Claretwood Finish	110–160	140	110–155	100–130	120–130	120–150	140
Glenmorangie Cognac Matured	140–155	140–170	110–135	100–110	110–180	100–160	160
Glenmorangie – 10-year-old (26 2/3 fl. oz)				53			40–55
Glenmorangie Dornoch Firth Bridge – 10-year-old				95	45–100	60–75	60
Glenmorangie Grand Slam Dram – 10-year-old (One of only 18 bottles with original signiatures)					550	420	
Glenmorangie Grand Slam Dram – 10-year-old	48–85	50–85	70	55–95	45–90	60–95	45–50
Glenmorangie Nat. Cask Strength – 10-year-old	48						
Glenmorangie – 10-year-old (75 cl.)	42					27–40	
Glenmorangie Cellar 13 – 10-year-old					20		30
Glenmorangie – 10-year-old (150th Anniversary)					50–130		
Glenmorangie Traditional – 10-year-old (57.2%)	60	70	30–120	30	40–70	30–40	35
Glenmorangie Cote De Beaune – 12-year-old (46%)						65	30–45
Glenmorangie Golden Rum Cask – 12-year-old (40%)							50
Glenmorangie Madeira Finish – 12-year-old			110				
Glenmorangie Port Wood – 12-year-old (46.5%)					70	75	
Glenmorangie Millennium Malt – 12-year-old (40%)				30	27	30–45	32–62
Glenmorangie Three Cask Matured – 12-year-old			100–110			50	
Glenmorangie Fino Sherry – 13-year-old (43%)			22–25				

Whisky Auction Sale Results (£s)	2000	2001	2002	2003	2004	2005	2006
Glenmorangie Fino Sherry – 14-year-old (43%)						42	
Glenmorangie Maltman's Vintage – 15-year-old			56				
Glenmorangie – 17-year-old – 1987							
(Limited edition of 346, bottled 2004, 56.4%)						320	
Glenmorangie – 18-year-old	48	40–50	56			42	
Glenmorangie Maltman's Reserve – 18-year-old	40	40		80	80–125		120
Glenmorangie Sauternes Wood – 20-year-old – 1981 (46%)							110–140
Glenmorangie Elegance – 21-year-old	105		70–85		80	105–140	150
Glenmorangie Sesquicentennial – 21-year-old	130–140		140–150	110–160	100–140	80–150	110–180
Glenmorangie – 21-year-old – 1977 (43%)				75	70		60–80

Left to right.
Glenmorangie Grand Slam Dram – 10-year-old,
Glenmorangie Sesquicentennial – 21-year-old,
Glenmorangie Millennium Malt – 12-year-old,
Glenmorangie Last Christmas At Leith

Whisky Auction Sale Results (£s)	2000	2001	2002	2003	2004	2005	2006
Glenmorangie – 22-year-old – 1963	240–260	240–340		210–280	290–310	260–285	290–360
Glenmorangie Malaga Wood – 25-year-old (43%)		80	60–80	45–80	70–90	50–55	80–130
Glenmorangie – 25-year-old (43%)						75	100
Glenmorangie Cotes De Nuits – 25-year-old – 1975 (43%)		150	100–120	110–140	130–170	180	190–230
Glenmorangie Single Barrel – 1971 (46%)		90	65				
Glenmorangie – 1971 (Rear labelled for 150th Anniversary)				90–100	80–150	105–170	100
Glenmorangie Culloden – 1971	100–110	100–115	115–160	125–200	110–200	145–180	130–190
Glenmorangie Single Barrel – 1972 (46%)		170			140		130
Glenmorangie – 1974 (43%)		110			45		
Glenmorangie Original – 1974	160	80–100		50		45–100	100
Glenmorangie – 1975 (43%)							60–70
Glenmorangie – 1975 (46.6%)		130					

Left to right.
Glenmorangie – 1971,
Glenmorangie Sauternes – 1981,
Glenmorangie – 1977

Whisky Auction Sale Results (£s)	2000	2001	2002	2003	2004	2005	2006
Glenmorangie Port Wood –1975 (46.8%)					220		
Glenmorangie – 1976 (Concorde flight, 60.4%)		630					
Glenmorangie – 1976 (Concorde flight, 59.2%)				550			
Glenmorangie Tain L'Hermitage – 28-year-old – 1975 (46%)					200	120–140	180
Glenmorangie Oloroso Cask – 30-year-old – (44.3%)							130–160
Glenmorangie Tain L'Hermitage – 1978	90	60–130	110–130	90	80–90		150
Glenmorangie – 1979 (40%)		50	22–30	22	45	32–40	40
Glenmorangie Native Ross-shire – 10-year-old – 1980 (58.4%)		90					
Glenmorangie Native Ross-shire – 10-year-old – 1980 (56.8%)						85	
Glenmorangie Native Ross-shire – 10-year-old – 1980 (58%)					60		
Glenmorangie Native Ross-shire – 10-year-old – 1980 (57.6%)					60–80		
Glenmorangie Native Ross-shire – 10-year-old – 1980 (59.6%)				100			
Glenmorangie Native Ross-shire – 10-year-old – 1981 (60.4%)					60		
Glenmorangie Native Ross-shire – 10-year-old – 1981 (59.6%)					60		
Glenmorangie Native Ross-shire – 10-year-old – 1981 (59.2%)					65–80		
Glenmorangie Dist. Man's Choice – 1981 (54.5%)		115–240	260		140–220		
Glenmorangie Native Ross-shire – 10-year-old – 1982 (59.2%)					85		

Whisky Auction Sale Results (£s)	2000	2001	2002	2003	2004	2005	2006
Glenmorangie Native Ross-shire – 10-year-old – 1982 (58%)					65		
Glenmorangie Native Ross-shire – 10-year-old – 1982 (58.4%)						80	
Glenmorangie Dist. Man's Choice – 1983 (53.2%)				220			
Glenmorangie Native Ross-shire – 10-year-old – 1983 (57.2%)					85		
Glenmorangie Sauternes – Over-20-year-old – 1981 (46%)						90–110	100–120
Glenmorangie Native Ross-shire – 10-year-old – 1983 (57.6%)					60		
Glenmorangie Native Ross-shire – 10-year-old – 1983 (58%)					65		
Glenmorangie Native Ross-shire – 10-year-old – 1984 (60.4%)		115					
Glenmorangie Dist. Man's Choice – 1987 (57.2%)			140				150–180
Glenmorangie Missouri Oak – 1991 (55.7%)							75
Glenmorangie Natural Cask – 1991 (57.7%)							30
Glenmorangie Burr Oak – 1993 (56.3%)							50
Glenmorangie Everest – 1993 (46%)				170	250		
Glenmorangie Speakeasy – 1990 (59.7%)					60		
Glenmorangie – 10-year-old – 1993 (Limited edition of 350, bottled 2003, 56.9%)						120–160	
Glenmorangie (Last Christmas, Leith, 1893–1993)	150		290–360	260	250–380	380	240–300

Glenrothes

This varied selection of expressions of Glenrothes has been offered at auction which includes distillery and independent bottlings

Whisky Auction Sale Results (&s)	2000	2001	2002	2003	2004	2005	2006
Glenrothes – Glenlivet – 8-year-old (26 2/3 fl. oz)			60–110	130	33–60		
Glenrothes – Glenlivet – 10-year-old (Cadenhead's, 80 degrees)						165	
Glenrothes – 10-year-old – 1989 (Hart Bros)		20					
Glenrothes – 12-year-old (Rear label 1989, 750 ml.)			45	45	52	42–60	
Glenrothes – 16-year-old – 1975 (Signatory, 43%)					40	90	
Glenrothes – 20-year-old – 1979 (Adelphi, 55.6%)		34					
Glenrothes – 21-year-old – 1975 (First Cask)		33			32	30	
Glenrothes – 22-year-old – 1957 (Cadenhead's)	90						

Glenrothes – 28-year-old – 1954

Whisky Auction Sale Results (£s)	2000	2001	2002	2003	2004	2005	2006
Glenrothes – 24-year-old – 1976 (Adelphi, 52.7%)							22
Glenrothes – 25-year-old – 1975 (Douglas Laing)					55	45–50	30
Glenrothes – 26-year-old – 1968 (First Cask)		60			60		
Glenrothes – 28-year-old – 1954 (G & M)			120				
Glenrothes – 28-year-old – 1969 (Signatory, 50.5%)	40						
Glenrothes – 29-year-old – 1955 (G & M)						180	
Glenrothes – 30-year-old – 1956 (G & M)				155			180
Glenrothes – 1956 (G & M)					75		
Glenrothes – 1967 (46.6%)						360	
Glenrothes – 31-year-old – 1969 (Hart Bros, 46.8%)				43			
Glenrothes – 31-year-old – 1969 (Coopers Choice, 46%)						55	
Glenrothes – 31-year-old (MWBH Bonding, Cumbria, 53.4%)			75				
Glenrothes – 33-year-old – 1969 (Hart Bros, 46.8%)					33		40
Glenrothes – 35-year-old – 1961 (G & M)							95
Glenrothes – 1972							95
Glenrothes Centenary – 1978 (G & M)	25				32		
Glenrothes – 1979 (Cask 13470, 55.3%)							580
Glenrothes – 1979		60	20–37	40	23–32		27–60
Glenrothes – 1981				27			
Glenrothes – 1982						55	
Glenrothes – 1984			20–37	25	32	27–55	40–60
Glenrothes – 1987		30				35	
Glenrothes – 1989							25–60
Glenrothes – 1992					40		

Glenskiach

This early 20th century cask sample bottling is the only expression of Glenskiach that has been sold at auction over the last two decades

Whisky Auction Sale Results (£s)	2000	2001	2002	2003	2004	2005	2006
Glenskiach – 1917 (sample bottle)		1200					

Glenskiach – 1917

Glenturret

The 1960's cask selections of Glenturret have performed well at auction recently, old distillery bottlings have been very popular too

Whisky Auction Sale Results (£s)	2000	2001	2002	2003	2004	2005	2006
Glenturret – Over 7-year-old (26 2/3 fl. oz, 75 degrees proof)			90	180			
Glenturret – Over-8-year-old (75 cl.)	37			45	50–110	57	130
Glenturret – 8-year-old (70 cl.)					37	50	
Glenturret Bicentenary – 8-year-old – 1975 (Flagon, 37.5cl, 43%)							170
Glenturret – 10-year-old (Distillery Reserve)						50	55
Glenturret – 12-year-old (75 cl.)			25		45–53	23	
Glenturret – Over-12-year-old (45.7%)					50–75		130

Left to right.
Glenturret – 8-year-old,
Glenturret – 12-year-old

Whisky Auction Sale Results (£s)	2000	2001	2002	2003	2004	2005	2006
Glenturret – 15-year-old – 1977 (50%)					80		
Glenturret – 15-year-old – 1981 (50%)			35	60			
Glenturret – 15-year-old (75 cl., 43%)					33	25	
Glenturret – 15-year-old (Gilt decanter, 40%)							155
Glenturret – 16-year-old – 1980 (Murray McDavid)	37						
Glenturret – 18-year-old (40%)					80		50
Glenturret – 18-year-old – 1976 (First Cask)			50				
Glenturret – 18-year-old – 1980 (Cadenhead's, 45.7%)						70	
Glenturret – 21-year-old (1494 – 1994)	155					280	
Glenturret – 21-year-old (Gilt flagon, 40%)				70	80	102	
Glenturret – 21-year-old – 1978 (First Cask)	45				34	30	
Glenturret – 25-year-old (Ceramic globe decanter)			80		80–140		
Glenturret – 27-year-old – 1978 (Mission Series 5, 46%)							38
Glenturret – 1965	190		270				
Glenturret – 1966 (45.7%)	80	110	155		150		
Glenturret Classic Vintage – 1966	75	90			150	102	260
Glenturret – 1966 (Gilt ceramic jug, 43%)		180–200	140	100			
Glenturret – 1967 (50%)	90						
Glenturret – 1972 (37.5 cl)		60					
Glenturret – 1972 (47%)					90	92	100–130
Glenturret – 1976	70						
Glenturret – 1979 (SMWS, 54.9%)					65		
Glenturret – 1980 (55.2%)					70	55	100

Glenugie

Older expressions of Glenugie have appeared at auction fetching healthy prices

Whisky Auction Sale Results (£s)	2000	2001	2002	2003	2004	2005	2006
Glenugie – 20-year-old (Crystal decanter)	220						
Glenugie – 12-year-old – 1966 (Cadenhead's, 45.7%)		170	55	67			
Glenugie – 12-year-old – 1980 (Cadenhead's. 59.8%)			37	45			
Glenugie – 13-year-old – 1978 (Cadenhead's. 60.9%)							37
Glenugie – 15-year-old – 1966 (G & M)						135	
Glenugie – 16-year-old – 1966 (G & M)		90				130	
Glenugie – 18-year-old – 1959 (Cadenhead's)		170					
Glenugie – 19-year-old – 1978 (Silent Stills, 57.4%)				80			
Glenugie – 23-year-old – 1965 (Hart Bros, 43%)			28		23		
Glenugie – 26-year-old – 1977 (46%)						48	42
Glenugie – 27-year-old – 1973 (Ian MacLeod, 54.2%)				50			
Glenugie – 30-year-old – 1966 (Signatory, 58%)			100				
Glenugie – 30-year-old – 1967 (G & M)				80			
Glenugie – 31-year-old – 1966 (Silent Stills)	52						
Glenugie – 33-year-old – 1966 (Italian import)	165						
Glenugie – 1966 (G & M)			32		35–75	37–80	
Glenugie – 1967 (G & M)	26					37–80	60
Glenugie – 1967 (Italian import)		160					
Glenugie – 1968 (G & M)				120	40	42	
Glenugie – 1978 (SMWS, 60%)					120		
Glenugie – 1980 (Cadenhead's, 58.1%)				50	73–82		

Glenury

These examples of Glenury listed are the only ones that have appeared at auction recently, the mature cask strength examples and older distillery bottlings attract the most interest

Whisky Auction Sale Results (£s)	2000	2001	2002	2003	2004	2005	2006
Glenury Royal – 12-year-old (J Gillon & Co)		190	110		130–190	105–215	120–145
Glenury – 14-year-old – 1978 (Signatory, 43%)			37				
Glenury Royal – 14-year-old – 1978 (Master of Malt, 43%)				40			
Glenury – 16-year-old – 1978 (Signatory, 43%)				27		30	
Glenury Royal – 23-year-old – 1966 (Cadenhead's, 53.8%)	320				105–110		
Glenury Royal – 23-year-old – 1971 (61.3%)	48	63	53		70	53–107	150
Glenury Royal – 24-year-old – 1973 (Silent Stills, 53.7%)			70				
Glenury Royal – 28-year-old – 1970 (58.4%)			80				
Glenury Royal – 29-year-old – 1970 (57%)		43			50–60		80
Glenury – 33-year-old – 1968 (Douglas Laing, 48.8%)						110	
Glenury – 34-year-old – 1968 (Douglas Laing, 43.4%)							110
Glenury – 1973 (SMWS, 52.8%)		60					50
Glenury Royal – 1976 (G & M)				43		24	60
Glenury Royal – 1978 (Captain Burns, 43%)					35		
Glenury – 1983 (SMWS, 63.1%)				50			

Grange

This rare early 20th century example is the only historical bottling from Grange Distillery that has been sold at auction over the last decade

Whisky Auction Sale Results (£s)	2000	2001	2002	2003	2004	2005	2006
O B Grange – Early 20th century (W Young & Co)		2000					

Highland Park

Some fine examples of Highland Park have come up at auction, older expressions attract great interest, as do the wide and varied range of bottlings, many at cask strength spanning a variety of years

Whisky Auction Sale Results (£s)	2000	2001	2002	2003	2004	2005	2006
Highland Park Reserve – 1902 (Berry Bros)	1500–2700						
Highland Park – 1906 (Matthew Gloag & Son)	420						
Highland Park – 1951 (Tall 75 cl., 43%)					290		
Highland Park – 1952 (G & M)			460		120–160	260	210
Highland Park – 1955 (G & M, 54.6%)			170				
Highland Park – 1955 (Berry Bros & Rudd)		180					
Highland Park – 1964 (G & M)					52		
Highland Park – 1967		100	95–110		150–180	190–195	
Highland Park – 1970 (G & M, centenary)					40		
Highland Park – 1971 (SMWS, 56%)		189					
Highland Park – 1974 (Online tasting, 52.6%)				240			
Highland Park – 1976 (SMWS, 58.8%)							100
Highland Park Bicentenary – 1977		70		70		110	120
Highland Park Vintage – 1977 (52.1%)						120–140	
Highland Park – 1978 (SMWS, 59.5%%)		189					
Highland Park – 1979 (SMWS, 55.2%)		60					
Highland Park – 1979 (Cadenhead's, 65.6%)			120				
Highland Park – 1980 (Maxium visit, 50.5%)				230			240
Highland Park – 1980 (SMWS, 56.3%)					50		
Highland Park – 1982 (G & M, 56.8%)					53		

Whisky Auction Sale Results (£s)	2000	2001	2002	2003	2004	2005	2006
Highland Park Vintage – 1986 (56.2%)						80–90	
Highland Park – 1988 (Danish bottling, 43%)				22			
Highland Park (No age, 26 2/3 fl. oz, 100 degrees)					340	360	420
Highland Park (No age, 26 2/3 fl. ozs., 75 degrees)							580
Highland Park Capella					110		
Highland Park – 8-year-old (26 2/3 fl. oz, 70 degrees proof)					160	150	160
Highland Park – 8-year-old (G & M, 26 2/3 fl. ozs)			90	50	75	65–110	65
Highland Park – 8-year-old (G & M, 57%)				50	50–60		
Highland Park – 8-year-old (Italian import)		80					
Highland Park – 10-year-old (Signatory, 43%)	42		50				27
Highland Park – 11-year-old – 1990 (Signatory, 58.1%)						35	
Highland Park 2000 – 12-year-old (200 bottles, 55.7%)					90–100	170–180	180
Highland Park – 12-year-old – Early 20th century (Stopper cork, lead capsule, 26 2/3 fl. oz, 70 degrees)				1100			
Highland Park – 12-year-old (Dumpy green, black & gilt labels)					93		
Highland Park Eunson's Legacy – 12-year-old (40%)			160–170	130			280
Highland Park – 12-year-old (75 cl.)				50	60	50–160	40
Highland Park – 12-year-old (Italian Royal visit)		180					
Highland Park – 12-year-old (Italian import)		110					
Highland Park – 13-year-old – 1974 (Italian import, 58.4%)	125						
Highland Park – 16-year-old – 1980 (Hart Bros, 43%)					38		
Highland Park – 17-year-old (Dumpy green, black & gilt labels)		100			93		

THE BEST SPIRIT IN THE WORLD

The basic process at Highland Park is similar to that at other distilleries but it is the differences rather than the similarities which contribute most to this classic single malt whisky. The quality of Highland Park is built on five fundamental keystones.

HAND-TURNED MALT adds to the deliciously succulent, balanced layers of aromatic character found in Highland Park single malt Scotch whisky.

AROMATIC PEAT gives a delectably seductive, luxuriant floral sweetness to Highland Park single malt Scotch whisky.

COOL MATURATION enhances the smooth character of Highland Park single malt Scotch whisky.

SHERRY OAK CASKS contribute to the distinctive richness and multi-dimensional complexity of Highland Park single malt Scotch whisky.

CASK HARMONISATION ensures consistency and balance in Highland Park single malt Scotch whisky.

The accolade of Best Spirit in the World was no fluke; it was based on an unbroken tradition of whisky-making stretching back at Highland Park to 1798. Highland Park is arguably the most respected single malt in the world. As everyone knows, respect has to be earned. More than 200 years of distilling tradition, attention to detail and honesty at Highland Park has achieved just that.

HIGHLAND PARK
SINGLE MALT SCOTCH WHISKY

American drinks guru F. Paul Pacult recently published a list of the top 100 spirits in the world. Sitting atop the list was Highland Park 18 Year Old.

Whisky Auction Sale Results (£s)	2000	2001	2002	2003	2004	2005	2006
Highland Park – 17-year-old – 1958 (Italian import)	90						
Highland Park – 17-year-old – 1960 (Italian import)	125						
Highland Park – 18-year-old (70 cl.)				32–37			
Highland Park – 18-year-old – 1976 (Cadenhead's, 62%)				63			
Highland Park – 18-year-old – 1979 (Murray McDavid, 46%)							25

Left to right. Highland Park (No age), Highland Park – 12-year-old, Highland Park – 25-year-old – 1941

Whisky Auction Sale Results (£s)	2000	2001	2002	2003	2004	2005	2006
Highland Park – 19-year-old – 1959 (Italian import)	170	175					
Highland Park – 19-year-old – 1975 (First Cask)		35					
Highland Park – 19-year-old – 1977 (Adelphi, 57.9%)							50
Highland Park – 20-year-old (26 2/3 fl. oz)	270						
Highland Park – 20-year-old – 1956 (Italian import)	90						
Highland Park – 20-year-old – 1962 (Blackadder)			37				
Highland Park – 20-year-old – 1974 (First Cask)		45			37	40	50
Highland Park – 20-year-old – 1975 (Signatory, 54.3%)				43			
Highland Park – 20-year-old – 1977 (Hart Bros, 43%)		25–35		47	25–37	36	32
Highland Park – 20-year-old – 1986 (Hart Bros, 46%)							30
Highland Park – 21-year-old (Dumpy green, black & gilt labels)					93		
Highland Park – 21-year-old – 1957 (Cadenhead's, 45.7%)	105			145	190		
Highland Park – 21-year-old – 1959 (Italian import)	90	80					
Highland Park – 21-year-old – 1975 (Signatory, 43%)							32
Highland Park – 22-year-old – 1961 (R W Duthie, 46%)				140			
Highland Park – 22-year-old – 1961 (Cadenhead's, 46%)					160		
Highland Park – 23-year-old – 1979 (Mission, Series 1, 46%)							40
Highland Park – 25-year-old (53.5%)	95		75			75	70–100
Highland Park – 25-year-old (G & M, Silver Jubilee)				150		210	120
Highland Park – 25-year-old – 1941 (26 2/3 fl. oz)	490						
Highland Park – 25-year-old – 1975 (Douglas Laing, 50%)							100
Highland Park – 27-year-old – 1972 (Douglas Laing, 50%)							100
Highland Park – 25-year-old – 1975 (Hart Bros, 43%)		35		47	40	36–37	32–35
Highland Park – 25-year-old – 1976 (First Cask)					35–52		

Whisky Auction Sale Results (£s)	2000	2001	2002	2003	2004	2005	2006
Highland Park – 25-year-old – 1979 (Mission, Series 4, 46%)							40
Highland Park – 26-year-old – 1973 (Adelphi, 54.6%)							50
Highland Park – 27-year-old – 1968 (Hart Bros)	42						
Highland Park – 28-year-old – 1973 (Cask 11151, 45.4%)				180	120–130	150–190	150
Highland Park – 28-year-old – 1973 (Cask 11167, 50.4%)				120–190	120–140	125–190	190–220
Highland Park – 28-year-old – 1974 (Douglas Laing, 56.8%)						70	90
Highland Park – 30-year-old – 1970 (Douglas Laing, 50%)				70–75	95		100
Highland Park – 35-year-old – 1955 (G & M, 52.8%)			320				
Highland Park – 35-year-old – 1966 (Hart Bros, 41.1%)				47			
Highland Park – 35-year-old – 1967 (Jim McEwan's Celtic Heartlands, 40.1%)						147	173
Highland Park – 37-year-old – 1965 (Scott's Selection, 42.2%)					130		
Highland Park – 40-year-old (Black ceramic)	470						980
Highland Park – 40-year-old – 1958 (44%)							1100–1550

Hillside

These expressions of Hillside listed are all examples from the Rare Malts Selection, with one exception

Whisky Auction Sale Results (£s)	2000	2001	2002	2003	2004	2005	2006
Hillside – 25-year-old – 1969 (61.9%)			105				
Hillside – 25-year-old – 1970 (60.1%)	40–155	35–50	77	32–50	67–80	53–110	120–140
Hillside – 25-year-old – 1971 (62%)	36		53		95		
Hillside – 28-year-old – 1971 (Silent Stills, 51.4%)	52						

Hillside – 25-year-old

Imperial

This small selection of expressions of Imperial have appeared at auction over the last few years

Whisky Auction Sale Results (£s)	2000	2001	2002	2003	2004	2005	2006
Imperial – 18-year-old – 1962 (Cadenhead's, 46%)						100–150	
Imperial – 1970 (G & M)	58		24–37		35		
Imperial – 17-year-old – 1970 (G & M)						90	
Imperial – 1976 (SMWS, 66.2%)		167				180	
Imperial Millennium – 1977 (Gall & Gall, 43%)					35		
Imperial – 1979 (G & M)			30		24–25	23–50	33
Imperial Calvados Finish – 1990 (G & M)		37			30	18–33	
Imperial Cognac Finish – 1990 (G & M)		37				18	20
Imperial Claret Finish – 1990 (G & M)		37				18	
Imperial Sherry Finish – 1990 (G & M)							20
Imperial Cognac Finish – 1991 (G & M)							20
Imperial Port Finish – 1991 (G & M)							20
Imperial – 15-year-old (Allied Distillers)			31		17–30	18–27	
Imperial – 15-year-old (James MacArthur, 43%)					17		
Imperial – 17-year-old – 1982 (Association of Deacons, Glasgow, 43%)				90			

Inchgower

These examples of Inchgower listed are the only ones that have appeared at auction recently, older distillery bottlings being the most popular

Whisky Auction Sale Results (£s)	2000	2001	2002	2003	2004	2005	2006
Inchgower – 12-year-old (75 cl.)	25	62	37	120	30–100	50–55	
Inchgower – 12-year-old (26 2/3 fl. oz)	70		40–70	50–70	62–110	50	70
Inchgower – 12-year-old (1 litre)		100					
Inchgower – 14-year-old (Flora & Fauna)	38		33	26–32	18–26		20–75
Inchgower – 17-year-old – 1959 (Cadenhead's, 46%)							70
Inchgower – 1966 (SMWS, 61.6%)					55		45
Inchgower – 18-year-old – 1976 (First Cask)		26					40
Inchgower – 22-year-old – 1970 (55.7%)				50			
Inchgower – 22-year-old – 1974 (55.7%)					42–57	75	50
Inchgower – 26-year-old – 1976 (Hart Bros, 49.9%)						23–32	43
Inchgower – 1977 (Cadenhead's, 59.2%)							60

Inchgower – 12-year-old

Isle of Jura

The first two entries are the only old historical examples of bottles from Jura Distillery to appear at auction over the last decade, cask strength recent and old distillery bottlings are popular too

Whisky Auction Sale Results (£s)	2000	2001	2002	2003	2004	2005	2006
Isle of Jura – Season 1882 (Charles R Haig)	4100	2100					
Jura (Cask 1124, 58.8%)							65
Isle of Jura – 8-year-old (75 cl.)			52–65	40–95	38–75		27
Isle of Jura – 8-year-old (26 2/3 fl. oz)			75	65–85		47	
Isle of Jura – 10-year-old (75 cl.)			52			33–80	30–25
Isle of Jura – 10-year-old (Litre)					37		
Isle of Jura – 10-year-old (Glass still shaped decanter)				55			
Isle of Jura – 10-year-old (57.2%)					35		
Isle of Jura – 13-year-old – 1992 (56.6%)							55
Isle of Jura – 20-year-old (54%)							100
Isle of Jura – 25-year-old (Stillman's Dram, 45%)			40		35	45	
Isle of Jura – 25-year-old – 1976 (Douglas Laing, 50%)					55	42–45	
Isle of Jura – 26-year-old (Stillman's Dram, 45%)		45		33	40		
Isle of Jura – 27-year-old (Stillman's Dram, 45%)				120		45	
Isle of Jura – 30-year-old – 1966 (Signatory, 56.2%)			75		110	90	
Isle of Jura – 30-year-old – 1973 (55%)							150–160
Isle of Jura – 32-year-old – 1966 (Signatory, 50.6%)			115		100		
Isle of Jura – 33-year-old – 1966 (Douglas Laing)						60	50
Isle of Jura – 36-year-old (44%)				140	280	190	240–380

Whisky Auction Sale Results (£s)	2000	2001	2002	2003	2004	2005	2006
Jura – Over 20-year-old – 1965 (Hand bottled for Jane Prosser, 56%)			260				
Jura – 1969 (Lord Astor, private bottling)			290	270	400	280	320
Isle of Jura – 1972 (SMWS, 55.5%)					100		
Jura – 1984 (George Orwell, 42%)						25–42	37
Isle of Jura Superstition (42%)						25	

Jura – 1969 (Lord Astor)

Kinclaith

Kinclaith never fails to fetch a good price when it make's it's appearance at auction

Whisky Auction Sale Results (£s)	2000	2001	2002	2003	2004	2005	2006
Kinclaith – 16-year-old – 1966 (G & M)	720			450	400		
Kinclaith – 20-year-old – 1965 (Cadenhead's, 46%)							420–580
Kinclaith – 1966 (G & M)		500					
Kinclaith – 1966 (G & M, miniature)			107				40–45
Kinclaith – 1967 (G & M, miniature)							30
Kinclaith – 1967 (G & M)		420	360–400	250–460	320–420	330	
Kinclaith – 1968 (G & M)		760	460–600	350			540
Kinclaith – 24-year-old (Cadenhead's, 18.75 cl., no age statement, 51.4%)					60		
Kinclaith – 24-year-old – 1965 (Cadenhead's Authentic Collection, 51.4%)				1500			
Kinclaith – 24-year-old – 1965 (Cadenhead's, brown, dumpy, bad level, 51.4%)						380	
Kinclaith – 26-year-old – 1975 (Signatory, 52.3%)			800	520–680			720
Kinclaith – 35-year-old – 1969 (signatory, 54%)						420	

Kinloch

This rare late 19th century example is the only historical bottling from Kinloch Distillery that has been sold at auction over the last decade and is one of the most expensive whiskies

Whisky Auction Sale Results (£s)	2000	2001	2002	2003	2004	2005	2006
Kinloch – 1880 (Lamb, Colville & Co)		5200					

Kinloch – 1880

Knockando

This varied and select range of vintage Knockando has appeared at auction recently

Whisky Auction Sale Results (£s)	2000	2001	2002	2003	2004	2005	2006
Knockando Extra Old Reserve (It's A Knockout)			120				
Knockando – 12-year-old – 1959 (Poor label)						200	
Knockando Extra Old Reserve – 1964	55					155	120
Knockando Extra Old Reserve – 1965					140	80–95	
Knockando Extra Old Reserve – 1966		35					
Knockando Extra Old Reserve – 1968			50–60		110	100	
Knockando Extra Old Reserve – 1969				100	215		
Knockando Extra Old Reserve – 1970							50
Knockando Extra Old Reserve – 1973				100			
Knockando – 12-year-old – 1963			40	105			
Knockando – 12-year-old – 1964			50				
Knockando – 12-year-old – 1965							55
Knockando – 12-year-old – 1966	50		35			27	
Knockando – 12-year-old – 1967		35					
Knockando – 12-year-old – 1980 (Cadenhead's, 58%)					43		
Knockando – 1970					32–65		
Knockando – 1971	43						
Knockando – 1972			63–70				
Knockando – 1973	27–42						
Knockando – 1974						20–85	
Knockando Single Cask – 21-year-old – 1973 (43%)					130		

Whisky Auction Sale Results (£s)	2000	2001	2002	2003	2004	2005	2006
Knockando Extra Old Reserve – 21-year-old – 1979 (43%)							70
Knockando – 20-year-old – 1974 (Aberdeen University Quincentenary)				100–170	65–70	70	55–80
Knockando – 1975					52–60		
Knockando – 1976					20	35	30
Knockando – 1977			35		33	43	37
Knockando Extra Old Reserve – 1977			47	30			
Knockando – 1978			20–30	20–30	33	38	
Knockando – 1978 (Private bottling, 1992)					80		
Knockando – 1979	43–55		20	25	17–33		
Knockando – 1982				20	30	43	
Knockando – 1983					32		50
Knockando – 1984						43–45	
Knockando Centenary – 1986		25	33	27–30	20–40		55
Knockando Centenary – 1986 (With decanter)	80				60	35–80	
Knockando – 1988					20		
Knockando – 1990							25

Knockando – 1978

Knockdhu

This small selection show the recent results of expressions from Knockdhu Distillery

Whisky Auction Sale Results (£s)	2000	2001	2002	2003	2004	2005	2006
An Cnoc – 12-year-old			32	17	28	18	
Knockdhu – 13-year-old – 1989 (46%)							30
Knockdhu – 12-year-old (75 cl.)		45	37	40	33	18	35
Knockdhu – 21-year-old (57.5%)		45–50	32		40		
Knockdhu – 11-year-old – 1974 (G & M)					40		
Knockdhu – 12-year-old – 1974 (G & M)				60			
Knockdhu – 1974 (G & M)			20–22	21–27	20–32		32
Knockdhu – 1974 (Scott's Selection, 63.6%)				33			
Knockdhu – 20-year-old – 1978 (Adelphi, 59.7%)						20	20
Knockdhu – 23-year-old (57.4%)							40–65

Ladyburn

A small but select range of Ladyburn has appeared at auction lately with early bottlings fetching high prices

Whisky Auction Sale Results (£s)	2000	2001	2002	2003	2004	2005	2006
Ladyburn – 12-year-old (Distillery bottling)	2600						
Ladyburn – 12-year-old (Cadenhead's, no age, low level, 45.7%)						200	
Ladyburn – 12-year-old – 1966 (Cadenhead's, 46%)						340	290
Ladyburn – 14-year-old – 1966 (Cadenhead's, 46%)		1200					520
Ladyburn – 14-year-old – 1966 (Cadenhead's, level, lower shoulder)					200		
Ladyburn – 20-year-old – 1966 (Cadenhead's, 46%)				620	250	350	
Ladyburn (Ayrshire) – 1970 (G & M)		90–110	80–110				110
Ladyburn – 27-year-old – 1973 (50.4%)		310–320	250	400		200–240	190–230

Ladyburn – 14-year-old
(Cadenhead's)

Lagavulin

Early 20th century expressions of Lagavulin have achieved the highest prices at auction and a rare distillery cask strength bottling of 11-year-old spirit achieved one of the highest prices for this brand

Whisky Auction Sale Results (£s)	2000	2001	2002	2003	2004	2005	2006
Lagavulin – Believed 1875			3800				
Lagavulin – Bonded 1909 (John Bisset & Co)	4200						
Lagavulin – Bonded 1909 (Half bottle, John Bisset & Co)		1550	900				
Lagavulin – 1914 (10 U.P.)			600				
Lagavulin – Believed Early 20th century (Mackie & Co., driven cork)			3300				
Lagavulin – 10-year-old – Early 20th century (Mackie & Co, spring cap)			1700				
Lagavulin – 10-year-old – Believed Early 20th century (Mackie & Co, driven cork)			2700				
Lagavulin – 15-year-old – Believed Early 20th century (Mackie & Co, driven cork)			3800				
Lagavulin – 10-year-old – 1988 (Italian import, 56%)			90–120				
Lagavulin – 11-year-old (61.5%)	1500						
Lagavulin – 12-year-old (Cream label, clear glass)	290–360		190–210	180–250	175–270	170–270	215–290
Lagavulin – 12-year-old (Cream label, green glass)	180–210		100–150	200			
Lagavulin – 12-year-old (70 cl., 57.8%)							20
Lagavulin – 12-year-old (70 cl., 58%)							20
Lagavulin – 12-year-old – 1988 (Hart Bros, 56.2%)					50		
Lagavulin – 13-year-old – 1984 (Murray McDavid)	47–86						

Whisky Auction Sale Results (£s)	2000	2001	2002	2003	2004	2005	2006
Lagavulin – 14-year-old – 1984 (Murray McDavid)	64–86	75					
Lagavulin – 14-year-old – 1984 (Acorn, 51.7%)			100	90			
Lagavulin – 1987 (SMWS, 55.8%)			60				
Lagavulin – 15-year-old (Ceramic jug)	360	250–320	165–230	190–310			210–300
Lagavulin – 16-year-old (75 cl.)				28	27–33		
Lagavulin – 1978 (Cadenhead's, 63.6%)					145		
Lagavulin – 1978 (Cadenhead's, 63.5%)						67	
Lagavulin – 19-year-old – 1979 (Murray McDavid)	64–86	75					45
Lagavulin – 24-year-old – 1979 (46%)						60	40

Left to right.
Lagavulin (Spring cap),
Lagavulin (Mackie & Co),
Lagavulin – 12-year-old

Whisky Auction Sale Results (£s)	2000	2001	2002	2003	2004	2005	2006
Lagavulin – 23-year-old – 1979 (Mission, Ser.1, 46%)							40
Lagavulin – 25-year-old (57.2%)						97–150	92–130
Lagavulin Double Matured – 1979	40–52		27–45			35	47
Lagavulin – 1980			40	20		33–70	70
Lagavulin – 1980 (SMWS, 63.3%)					240		
Lagavulin – 1980 (SMWS, 63.8%)					135		
Lagavulin – 1981 (SMWS, 62.9%)					125		
Lagavulin – 1984 (SMWS, 62%)					130		
Lagavulin – 1984						35	
Lagavulin – 1986					36		40
Lagavulin – 1987 (SMWS, 55.8%)					85		
Lagavulin – 1987							47
Lagavulin – 1988						33	
Lagavulin – 1989							25–32

Laphroaig

Some fine examples of Laphroaig have appeared at auction, older expressions have attracted much interest, as have the wide and varied range of bottlings, many at cask strength spanning various years

Whisky Auction Sale Results (£s)	2000	2001	2002	2003	2004	2005	2006
Laphroaig Old Liqueur – Early 20th century (80 degrees)				700			
Laphroaig Reserve – 1902 (Berry Bros & Rudd)	2700					1500	
Laphroaig – Bottled 1903 (Mackie & Co)	3100						
Laphroaig Reserve – 1903 (Berry Bros & Rudd)	1450						
Laphroaig (Leapfrog) – 10-year-old (46%)				35	35		25–32
Laphroaig – 10-year-old (75 cl.)	50	95	100	40–43	50–75	65–80	55–140
Laphroaig – 10-year-old (26 2/3 fl. oz)	210		97–160	360	160–190	190	180–300

Left to right.
Laphroaig – 15-year-old-1970 (G & M),
Laphroaig – Vintage 1976

Whisky Auction Sale Results (£s)	2000	2001	2002	2003	2004	2005	2006
Laphroaig – 10-year-old (50cl. double pack)		105	80				
Laphroaig Royal Warrant – 10-year-old	170–190	110–220	205–240	100–150	120–130		125–340
Laphroaig – 10-year-old (Ian Henderson retirment)					250–260		
Laphroaig – 10-year-old (ISO 14001 achievement)					290	130	
Laphroaig Original Cask – 10-year-old (57.3%)							21
Laphroaig – 11-year-old (Islay Whisky Festival, 2003)					140–180	110–140	
Laphroaig – 12-year-old (Stone jug)	160						
Laphroaig – Over 12-year-old (Cadenhead's)		500					
Laphroaig – 13-year-old – 1984	90						
Laphroaig – 13-year-old – 1973 (G & M)					190		
Laphroaig Highgrove Edition – 1989			70	63		65	130
Laphroaig Highgrove Edition – 1990				63			

Left to right.
Laphroaig – 10-year-old,
Laphroaig Old Liqueur – Early 20th Century

Whisky Auction Sale Results (£s)	2000	2001	2002	2003	2004	2005	2006
Laphroaig Highgrove Edition – 1991				63			
Laphroaig – 15-year-old (75 cl.)	53–130	95	65		35–60	27	37
Laphroaig – 15-year-old (Macmillan Cancer Relief)				200	110		
Laphroaig Royal Warrant – 15-year-old			220	320			150
Laphroaig – 15-year-old – 1967 (Cadenhead's)							195
Laphroaig – 15-year-old – 1970 (G & M)		240–320			160		
Laphroaig – 16-year-old – 1970 (Italian import)			150				
Laphroaig – 17-year-old (Islay Whisky Festival, 2004)						190	
Laphroaig – 1975 (SMWS, 50.6%)					150		
Laphroaig – 19-year-old – 1969 (Italian import)			150				
Laphroaig – 26-year-old – 1968 (Hart Bros, 43%)					75	220	
Laphroaig – 27-year-old – 1967 (Signatory, 48.8%)		80	87				
Laphraoig – 27-year-old – 1967 (Signatory, 49.8%)						220	
Laphroaig – 27-year-old – 1967 (Signatory, 49%%)					115		
Laphroaig – 28-year-old – 1967 (Signatory, 50.2%)	150		100	160			
Laphroaig – 30-year-old		130	110–260		180	120–160	150–270
Laphroaig – 30-year-old – 1966 (Signatory, 48.6%)	130	100			115–190		
Laphroaig – 30-year-old – 1966 (Signatory, 48.7%)		95					
Laphroaig – 30-year-old – 1966 (Signatory, 48.9%)				75			
Laphroaig Vintage Reserve – 1960 (42.4%)		480	380	320–480	400–440	260–580	700–800
Laphroaig – 40-year-old – 1960 (43.4%)					300	450	420–680
Laphroaig Vintage – 1976		130			120–130	140	190
Laphroaig Vintage – 1977					170	160	260
Laphroaig – 1990 (Italian import, 45%)	67						

Ledaig

These are the only examples of Ledaig that have made an appearance at auction recently

Whisky Auction Sale Results (&s)	2000	2001	2002	2003	2004	2005	2006
Ledaig Tobermory – 6-year-old – 1972 (G & M)						100	
Ledaig – 13-year-old – 1972 (G & M)						90	
Ledaig – 13-year-old – 1973 (G & M)					100		
Ledaig Vintage – 1974		50	25–55	85	30–77		27–50
Ledaig – 1975 (SMWS, 51.2%)						90	
Ledaig – 1975 (Blackadder, 56.5%)		38					
Ledaig – 1978 (SMWS, 60.2%)						90	
Ledaig Vintage – 1979				35	30		27
Ledaig – 1990 (G & M)				20			
Ledaig – 20-year-old			25–35	70	40–55	55	25–27

Left to right.
Ledaig – 1974,
Ledaig – 1979,
Ledaig – 20-year-old

Linkwood

Mature Linkwood bottled in the 1970's and 1980's has proved very popular at auction in addition to the recently released Manager's Drams

Whisky Auction Sale Results (£s)	2000	2001	2002	2003	2004	2005	2006
Linkwood – Glenlivet – 1898 (Ian Grant & Co)					900		
Linkwood (G & M)			47		70		30
Linkwood – 10-year-old (Signatory, 43%)					27		
Linkwood – 12-year-old (Manager's Dram)	75–175	82–112	50–80	40–63	45–115	40–60	67–100
Linkwood – 12-year-old (Flora & Fauna)	38		20–35	27–48	32		38–50
Linkwood – 12-year-old (J McEwan & Co, 26 2/3 fl. oz)			85		170–190	80	
Linkwood – 12-year-old (J McEwan & Co, 75 cl)				40–50	140		95–115
Linkwood – 1946 (G & M)		240					
Linkwood – 1938 (Crystal decanter, G & M)		320					
Linkwood – 1938 (G & M)						220	
Linkwood – 1939 (G & M)		250					
Linkwood – Glenlivet – 1969 (Cadenhead's)			160				
Linkwood – 12-year-old – 1971 (J McEwan & Co)	27–42				90		120
Linkwood – 12-year-old – 1972 (J McEwan & Co)		70		45			55
Linkwood – 13-year-old – 1984 (Adelphi, 59.2%)							20
Linkwood – 13-year-old – 1990 (Adelphi, 56%)					45		
Linkwood – 14-year-old (Italian import, 40%)						55	
Linkwood – 15-year-old (Italian import, 60.8%)						55	
Linkwood – 17-year-old – Pre 1971 (J McEwan & Co)			95				120
Linkwood – 17-year-old – 1982 (Adelphi, 64.2%)						32	22
Linkwood – 20-year-old – 1975 (First Cask)			33				

Whisky Auction Sale Results (£s)	2000	2001	2002	2003	2004	2005	2006
Linkwood – 21-year-old – 1956 (Cadenhead's)		150					
Linkwood – 21-year-old – 1972 (First Cask)		27					
Linkwood – 25th Anniversary Burghead Maltings	310–550						280
Linkwood – 22-year-old – 1972 (59.3%)					57		60
Linkwood – 22-year-old – 1983 (Mission Selection 5, 46%)							38
Linkwood – 23-year-old – 1972 (58.4%)	36	65				55–77	75
Linkwood – 23-year-old – 1974 (61.2%)			57–77	37–60	60–67		47–65

 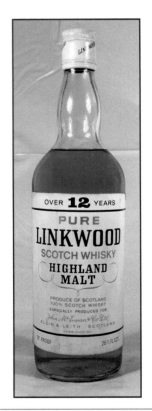

Left to right.
Linkwood – Glenlivet – 1898,
Linkwood – 12-year-old

Whisky Auction Sale Results (£s)	2000	2001	2002	2003	2004	2005	2006
Linkwood – 25-year-old (G & M)					55		
Linkwood – 25-year-old – 1960 (Italian import, glass decanter)	180–340	180–300					140
Linkwood – 27-year-old – 1974 (First Cask)							50
Linkwood – 1983 (59.8%)			25				
Linkwood – 1988 (43%)					32		
Linkwood – 29-year-old – 1973 (Mission Selection 2, 46%)							42
Linkwood – 36-year-old – 1946 (G & M)		130		170			
Linkwood – 37-year-old – 1939 (G & M)	230–290						190
Linkwood – 40-year-old (Italian import, crystal decanter)	230						
Linkwood – 40-year-old – 1946 (Italian import, glass decanter)		250				240	
Linkwood – 43-year-old – 1939 (G & M)		260					270
Linkwood – 44-year-old – 1938 (G & M)		150–190		225	200	220–250	
Linkwood – 45-year-old – 1938 (Sestante, G & M)	185	250–260					
Linkwood – 48-year-old (Italian import, crystal decanter)	500	450					
Linkwood – 48-year-old – 1939 (Sestante, G & M)	310	350					
Linkwood – 48-year-old (Sestante)		220–300					
Linkwood – 1954 (G & M)					100		
Linkwood – 1961 (G & M)					75		

Linlithgow

This rare bottling from Linlithgow by Matthew Gloag & Son is the only historical example sold at auction recently in addition to the independent bottlings listed

Whisky Auction Sale Results (£s)	2000	2001	2002	2003	2004	2005	2006
Linlithgow – 1891 (Matthew Gloag & Son)		1550					
Linlithgow – 9-year-old – 1982 ((Cadenhead's, 62.6%)					43		
Linlithgow – 17-year-old – 1982 (Signatory, 43%)					37		35
Linlithgow – 1982 (Cadenhead's, 65.4%)					100		
Linlithgow – 22-year-old – 1975 (Silent Stills, 51.7%)				75			
Linlithgow – 24-year-old – 1975 (Adelphi, 58.7%)							22
Linlithgow – 24-year-old – 1975 (First Cask, 46%)					28	25	
Linlithgow – 24-year-old – 1975 (Signatory, 51.5%)							60–70
Linlithgow – 26-year-old – 1974 (Douglas Laing)						25	50
Linlithgow – 29-year-old – 1975 (Mission Selection 4, 46%)							40
Linlithgow – 31-year-old – 1970 (Douglas Laing, 52.4%)						130	100
Linlithgow – 1982 (Cadenhead's, 64.3%)						100	

Linlithgow – 1891
(Matthew Gloag)

Littlemill

This small selection of Littlemill has made an appearance at auction, older bottlings though have fetched respectable sums

Whisky Auction Sale Results (£s)	2000	2001	2002	2003	2004	2005	2006
Littlemill – 5-year-old (26.4 fl. oz)	85		77				
Littlemill – 5-year-old (75cl.)					30		
Littlemill – 5-year-old (Italian import)		100					
Littlemill – 8-year-old (26.4 fl. oz)		30–80	40		53		23–40
Littlemill – 8-year-old (70 cl.)			43		20–27		23
Littlemill – 8-year-old – 1989 (Cadenhead's, 62.4%)							30
Littlemill – 12-year-old (54%)	70	55–120					
Littlemill – 12-year-old – 1984 (Signatory, 43%)							25
Littlemill – 18-year-old – 1975 (Signatory, 55.8%)			60				
Littlemill – 20-year-old – 1983 (First Cask)							50
Littlemill – 1975			65				
Littlemill – 1977 (SMWS, 48.8%)					80		
Littlemill – 30-year-old (40%)						120	
Littlemill – 30-year-old – 1950 (Stone jug, 53.5%)			260				
Littlemill – 30-year-old (Italian import)	150	100	150				
Littlemill – 31-year-old – 1965 (Silent Stills, 46.5%)						110	
Littlemill – 32-year-old – 1965 (Signatory, 49.1%)					65	55	
Littlemill – 34-year-old – 1965 (Douglas Laing, 43.9%)		80	85–90				52

Loch Lomond

This small selection of Loch Lomond has been sold with success at auction recently, the copper and glass lined decanter listed below fetching the highest price

Whisky Auction Sale Results (£s)	2000	2001	2002	2003	2004	2005	2006
Inchmurrin (75 cl.)				35	32	27	18
Old Rossdhu (75 cl.)				35–40	32	27	
Inchmurrin – 1966	80–90	90	75				60
Old Rossdhu – 1967				50–55			40–60
Inchmurrin – 1973 (G & M)							60
Loch Lomond – 23-year-old – 1974			65			60	70–90
Old Rossdhu – 24-year-old – 1979 (46%)						50	
Loch Lomond – 32-year-old – 1966 (Copper decanter, 47%)						420	

Lochindaal

This is the only historical example of a bottle from Lochindaal Distillery to appear at auction over the last decade

Whisky Auction Sale Results (&s)	2000	2001	2002	2003	2004	2005	2006
Lochindaal – bottled 1907 (J Bisset & Co)		2500					

Lochside

A small and interesting selection of Lochside has made it's appearance at auction recently

Whisky Auction Sale Results (£s)	2000	2001	2002	2003	2004	2005	2006
Lochside – 10-year-old (75 cl.)	95	70–140	60–95	67–120	100–120	90–130	135–140
Lochside – 17-year-old – 1965 (G & M)			90			90	
Lochside – 18-year-old – 1981 (Murray McDavid)	37						
Lochside – 20-year-old – 1965 (G & M)		140–150					
Lochside – 21-year-old – 1979 (Douglas Laing, 50%)				45			
Lochside – 22-year-old – 1966 (Signatory)	180–190						
Lochside – 23-year-old – 1981 (Cadenhead's, 47.7%)						130	
Lochside – 23-year-old – 1981 (Cadenhead's, 55.1%)							40–60
Lochside – 27-year-old (J MacArthur, 60.5%)						100	
Lochside – 1966 (G & M)		70	35–65		36–80		
Lochside – 31-year-old – 1959 (Signatory, 57.9%)			160–170		150		
Lochside – 31-year-old – 1962 (Cadenhead's, 56.7%)					90–100		
Lochside – 31-year-old – 1966 (Silent Stills, 57.7%)			120		120	110	
Lochside – 35-year-old – 1966 (Douglas Laing, 50%)					60	80	
Lochside – 37-year-old – 1966 (J Weibers, 47.7%)						85–130	
Lochside – 1981 (G & M)			40			40	31–100
Lochside – 1981 (Murray McDavid)					38		
Lochside – 1991 (G & M)							35

Longmorn

Some fine examples of Longmorn have appeared at auction including older expressions and a small selection of cask strength bottlings spanning various years

Whisky Auction Sale Results (£s)	2000	2001	2002	2003	2004	2005	2006
Longmorn – 1926 (Matthew Gloag & Son)	320						
Longmorn Glenlivet – Bonded March 1939 (Mayor Sworder & Co)	250–390	175–220					
Longmorn – Glenlivet – 1956 (G & M)		100					
Longmorn – 1962 (G & M)					45		
Longmorn – 1974 (Italian import, 46%)			122				
Longmorn – Glenlivet – 10-year-old	25						
Longmorn – Glenlivet – 10-year-old (75 cl.)		90–100				75	160
Longmorn – Glenlivet – 10-year-old (Hill Thomson, 26 2/3 fl. oz)			45–110				
Longmorn – Glenlivet – 12-year-old (75 cl.)			50		33–45	30	37
Longmorn – 15-year-old (75 cl.)			50	40–70	37–70	50	24
Longmorn – Glenlivet – 16-year-old – 1964 (Cadenhead's, 45.7%)						140	
Longmorn – Glenlivet – 19-year-old – 1974 (Cadenhead's, 45%)							30
Longmorn – 21-year-old – 1973 (First Cask)		73				40	
Longmorn – 23-year-old – 1972 (Signatory, 56.6%)				43			
Longmorn – 24-year-old – 1955 (G & M)				150			
Longmorn Centenary – 25-year-old (45%)		220–320	160–320				350

Whisky Auction Sale Results (£s)	2000	2001	2002	2003	2004	2005	2006
Longmorn – 25-year-old – 1958 (G & M)	43						
Longmorn – 25-year-old – 1960 (G & M)							140
Longmorn – 26-year-old – 1958 (G & M)				140			
Longmorn – Glenlivet – 1963 (G & M)					75		80
Longmorn – 30-year-old – 1964 (Signatory, 53.2%)		80					
Longmorn – 30-year-old – 1964 (Signatory, 43%)			75		120		
Longmorn – 30-year-old – 1969 (Adelphi, 56.7%)							73
Longmorn – 32-year-old – 1969 (Coopers' Choice, 56%)			110	70	60–80	47	
Longmorn – Glenlivet – 35-year-old – 1968 (Scott's Selection, 61.3%)							90
Longmorn – 1972 (SMWS, 61.7)							125–140
Longmorn – 1973 (SMWS, 57.9%)		189					
Longmorn – 1973 (G & M, 55.8%)						80	45
Longmorn – 1976 (SMWS, 59.8%)		60			70		
Longmorn – 1978 (SMWS, 56%)			47				

Longrow

Some fine examples of Longrow have appeared at auction including a rare old expression of '1864' and a sought after selection of cask strength bottlings from the 1970s and 1980s

Whisky Auction Sale Results (£s)	2000	2001	2002	2003	2004	2005	2006
Longrow – 15-year-old – 1864 (Beith Ross & Co)		7200					
Longrow – 8-year-old – 1987 (Signatory, 43%)	116	115	40–110	50	37		
Longrow – 9-year-old – 1987 (Signatory, 43%)	116				60	30	
Longrow – 9-year-old – 1990 (SMWS, 58.1%)							140
Longrow – 9-year-old – 1992 (Cadenhead's, 57.2%)							87
Longrow – 10-year-old (70 cl.)	70		40–70	40–45	55–100		37–55
Longrow Sherry Wood (70 cl.)							37
Longrow – 10-year-old – 1987 (Signatory, 43%)	116						87

Left to right.
Longrow – 14-year-old,
Longrow – 18-year-old – 1974

Whisky Auction Sale Results (£s)	2000	2001	2002	2003	2004	2005	2006
Longrow – 10-year-old – 1991							55
Longrow – 10-year-old – 1992				57			53
Longrow – 11-year-old – 1993 (Cadenhead's, 54.1%)							50
Longrow – 13-year-old – 1989 (53.2%)				70–100	60–100	55	40–53
Longrow – 14-year-old (70 cl., 46%)							30–35
Longrow – 14-year-old (75 cl., 46%)					1300		
Longrow – 16-year-old – 1974	200–260				150–300		
Longrow – 18-year-old – 1974 (Cadenhead's, 52.2%)					520–700		
Longrow – 19-year-old (Cask 1548)		1700					
Longrow – 21-year-old – 1974 (Cask 1549)			260				
Longrow – 25-year-old – 1974	260	330–340	270–350		260–300		
Longrow – 1973 (Small lettering)	270	280		270			
Longrow – 1973 (Large lettering)	400	470–480					
Longrow – 1973 (1st distillation, last cask, 43.2%)		460		620			
Longrow – 1974 Bond Reserve			380	320	300		
Longrow – 1982 (Blackadder, 58.9%)			70				
Longrow – 1987 (Italian import, 55%)			155				
Longrow – 1987 (Italian import, 55%)	130						
Longrow – 1987 (Italian import, 45%)	130						
Longrow – 1992 (Cadenhead's, 57.2%)					65		
Longrow – 1992 (56.8%)						47	35

The Macallan

The Macallan, over all the single malts, has held the world record auction hammer price for the longest, over an 18-year period. The most recent and highest price paid for a single bottle of The Macallan of any age at auction is currently £18,000, paid in 2002 and remained the world record until December of the same-year. However, in 2006 the distillers sold a bottle of 1926 for an amazing £35,000 to a private client. The vast range of bottlings that have appeared at auction over the years are the most varied of all the other expressions released by any other single malt distillery

Whisky Auction Sale Results (£s)	2000	2001	2002	2003	2004	2005	2006
Macallan (Campbell, Hope & King)					60		
Macallan – Glenlivet (Cadenhead's, low level)					45		
Macallan – Glenlivet As We Get It (57.3%)						40	
Macallan – Glenlivet As We Get It (59.9%)							65
Macallan – Glenlivet – 1872		2000					
Macallan – Glenlivet – 1879 (R Kemp, half)	600						
Macallan – Glenlivet – 31-year-old – 1879	3100			1300			
Macallan Rare Reserve – Distilled 1886	3400						
Macallan – 1890		1750					
Macallan – Glenlivet – 17-year-old – 1894		1750					
Macallan – Glenlivet – 19-year-old – 1892	1450						
Macallan Special Reserve – 1901 (R H Thomson)			1500				
Macallan – Glenlivet – Late 19th Century	3700						
Macallan – Glenlivet – Late 19th Century (J G Thomson)	1900						
Macallan – 60-year-old – 1926 (Unlabelled)		15,000	18,000				
Macallan – 60-year-old – 1926 (Adami label)				10,500			
Macallan – Glenlivet – 1927	2600						
Macallan – 50-year-old – 1928		4000	5200	3000–4600	4500–4600		4400–6000

Whisky Auction Sale Results (£s)	2000	2001	2002	2003	2004	2005	2006
Macallan – 50-year-old Millennium Decanter – 1949			1000–1700	920		1600	1700–1800
Macallan – 52-year-old – 1946	1050–1200	850–950	1500	750		850–880	1200
Macallan – 52-year-old – 1950 (51.7%)			1700				
Macallan – Glenlivet Horae Solaris	70						
Macallan – 'The 1841'				60–65		100	60–90
Macallan – 'The 1861'					60	55–100	70–100
Macallan – 'The 1874'	140–210	190–220	130–180	190–280	80–200	150–230	160–200
Macallan – 'The 1871'				50–70			
Macallan Excise Officers Dram (25 cl.)	18	20	15				
Macallan – 7-year-old		70	70				45–50
Macallan – 8-year-old (75 cl.)							100
Macallan Cask Strength – 10-year-old (58.8%)							45

Left to right.
Macallan – 7-year-old,
Macallan Private Eye,
Macallan – 1861 Replica,
Macallan – 1874 Replica

COLLECTING MALT WHISKY - A PRICE GUIDE

Whisky Auction Sale Results (£s)	2000	2001	2002	2003	2004	2005	2006
Macallan – 10-year-old (100 proof)	80		70		52–65	40	
Macallan – 10-year-old (G & M, 70 degrees)							95
Macallan – 10-year-old (75 cl.)				43	55–130	110	
Macallan – 10-year-old (Whisky Connoisseur, 40%)							75
Macallan – 10-year-old (Campbell, Hope & King, 70 degrees)				140			
Macallan – 10-year-old (51st Battalion)		410					
Macallan – 10-year-old (Knockando Church)	95–150	180–250	130–140			230	
Macallan – 10-year-old (Hall & Bramley)	500						
Macallan – 10-year-old (Speaker Martin's, 40%)							90
Macallan – 11-year-old (Whisky Connoisseur)						50	
Macallan – 12-year-old (French Revolution)	115–120	180					

Left to right.
Macallan – 1946,
Macallan – 1947,
Macallan – 1950,
Macallan – 1951,
Macallan – 1952

THE MACALLAN FINE & RARE
A COLLECTION WITHOUT EQUAL

Launched in 2002, The Macallan Fine & Rare is an unparalleled collection of vintage Macallan which tells the story of The Macallan in 40 *stunning chapters* from 1926 to 1976.

Carefully chosen for supreme *quality and rarity*, Fine & Rare enables collectors and connoisseurs to celebrate or mark *a special year* with the world's most precious vintage whisky.

www.themacallan.com

Whisky Auction Sale Results (&s)	2000	2001	2002	2003	2004	2005	2006
Macallan – 12-year-old (Jet Stream)			300			480	
Macallan – 12-year-old (3 litre bottle)				350			
Macallan – 12-year-old – 1988 (Adelphi, 57.7%)							20
Macallan – 12-year-old – 1990 (Moray 100th Open)							130
Macallan – Glenlivet – 15-year-old (Old G & M)	760		180–280	130			
Macallan – Glenlivet – 15-year-old		140					
Macallan Nicol's Nectar							580–800
Macallan Private Eye	70–155	90–160	90–140	130–210	140–200	180–230	190–240
Macallan Royal Marriage	320–360	270–360	240–340	320–480	400–580	310–480	420–650
Macallan Royal Marraige (Low spirit level)			200				
Macallan Special Reserve (75. cl.)	100–180	380		220			210–220
Macallan Special Reserve (70 cl.)			155				330

Left to right.
Macallan – 1938,
Macallan-Glenlivet – 1937,
Macallan – 25-year-old

Whisky Auction Sale Results (£s)	2000	2001	2002	2003	2004	2005	2006
Macallan – Glenlivet (Cadenhead's)	260			340			
Macallan – Glenlivet – 30-year-old – 1939	250–280						
Macallan – Glenlivet – 31-year-old – 1938	280–680						
Macallan – Glenlivet – 32-year-old – 1937	290–410	300	400				
Macallan – Glenlivet – 32-year-old – 1945	210						
Macallan – Glenlivet – 33-year-old	190	170					
Macallan – Glenlivet – 33-year-old – 1940	250						
Macallan – Glenlivet – 33-year-old – 1942						460	
Macallan – Glenlivet – 33-year-old – 1945	350	360					
Macallan – Glenlivet – 33-year-old – 1947		450					
Macallan – Glenlivet – 34-year-old – 1942	600						
Macallan – Glenlivet – 34-year-old – 1937	300	250					

Left to right.
Macallan – 60-year-old – 1926
(Adami label),
Macallan Jet Stream,
Macallan Royal Marriage

Whisky Auction Sale Results (£s)	2000	2001	2002	2003	2004	2005	2006
Macallan – Glenlivet – 35-year-old – 1937	300–500	250–310					
Macallan – 37-year-old – 1937 (43%)						1400	
Macallan – Glenlivet – 35-year-old – 1938	310						
Macallan – Glenlivet – 35-year-old – 1940	600	250–260					
Macallan – Glenlivet – 36-year-old – 1937	320	260					
Macallan – Glenlivet – 37-year-old – 1937	340–550						
Macallan – Glenlivet – 37-year-old – 1940	300		350				
Macallan – Glenlivet – 1937	180–460		420	520	480–550	210–550	360–420
Macallan – Glenlivet – 1937 (Low spirit level)			165		220		250
Macallan – Glenlivet – 39-year-old – 1941		630	500			460	
Macallan – Glenlivet – 40-year-old	400	300	350				
Macallan – Glenlivet – 1936		600					500
Macallan – 1936	450	480				470	
Macallan – 1937	440	260–400				470	360–420
Macallan – 1938	440	400				460	
Macallan – 1938 (Boxed)		650–820	620–700	480–720		380–800	750–900
Macallan – 1938 (Boxed, low spirit level)							420
Macallan – 1939	440	400				470	
Macallan – 1940	290–780	300–410				460	
Macallan – 1940 (Boxed, bottled 1981)			560				
Macallan – 1940 (Speymalt, G & M)						300	
Macallan – Glenlivet – 1942 (G & M)							340
Macallan – 1946	500	400–450	500		480–560	550–620	
Macallan – 1947	380–390	380–500	440		690	500–650	450
Macallan – 1948 (46.6%)		1150	1100–1700		800–900	800	2400

Whisky Auction Sale Results (£s)	2000	2001	2002	2003	2004	2005	2006
Macallan – 1948 (Miniature, 46.6%)				200			
Macallan – 40-year-old – 1949 (Signatory)		1150			380		
Macallan – Glenlivet – 30-year-old – 1950 (Boxed)	640						
Macallan – Vintage 1950 (Speymalt, G & M)		280					320–330
Macallan – 1950 (Campbell, Hope & King)					550	480	
Macallan – 1950 (Boxed)	640	240–420	330	210–620	270–520	370–460	460–580
Macallan – 1951		310				460–480	
Macallan Vintage – 1951 (48.8%)						500	
Macallan Vintage – 1951 (Miniature)							120
Macallan – 1952						430–520	
Macallan – 1954						380–430	380
Macallan – 1955	220					350–420	280–360
Macallan – 1956				150–230		290–360	380–560
Macallan – 1957 (G & M)					260	320–360	
Macallan – 1958	115–200			220	190	160–340	250–380
Macallan – 1959	150–220					260–340	220
Macallan – 1960	135–190	160	160			240	270
Macallan – 1961	160–180	150		160		190–200	
Macallan Vintage – 1961 (54.1%)				550		570–720	
Macallan Vintage – 1961 (Miniature)							100
Macallan – 1961 (Mitchell & Craig)	260						
Macallan – 1962 (Mitchell & Craig)	220						
Macallan – 1962					190	200–210	200
Macallan – 1963	75–150	110–160	80–130	110–340	190	140	
Macallan – 1963 (Northern Scot)		800					

Whisky Auction Sale Results (£s)	2000	2001	2002	2003	2004	2005	2006
Macallan – 1964	80–165	100–130	130	130–180	160–180		140
Macallan – 1965		140			170	130	150
Macallan – Glenlivet – 15-year-old – 1961		200					
Macallan – 1966 (SMWS, 56%)					110		
Macallan – 1966 (Speymalt, G & M)						110	130–170
Macallan – Glenlivet – 15-year-old – 1962	290						
Macallan – 17-year-old – 1965		140			130		
Macallan – 18-year-old – 1965			180	130			
Macallan – 18-year-old – 1966				190	130	150	175–190
Macallan – 18-year-old – 1967	35–50					130	130
Macallan – 18-year-old – 1968	35–50			90–110		100	165–180
Macallan – 18-year-old – 1969						100	
Macallan – 18-year-old – 1970	35				150	85	95
Macallan – 18-year-old – 1971	28–50				52–70	100	
Macallan – 18-year-old – 1972	35						50
Macallan – 18-year-old – 1973	35			90–110	55		
Macallan – 18-year-old – 1974	35			120	60–95	40–95	
Macallan – 18-year-old – 1974 (With goblets)	75–115	60–70					
Macallan – 18-year-old – 1975	20–26				75		
Macallan – 18-year-old – 1976	20–55				105		75
Macallan – 18-year-old – 1977	26–28				100–76		100
Macallan – 18-year-old – 1978					65		
Macallan – 18-year-old – 1979					76		70
Macallan – 18-year-old – 1983						65	
Macallan – 18-year-old – 1984					37		

Whisky Auction Sale Results (£s)	2000	2001	2002	2003	2004	2005	2006
Macallan Gran Reserva – 18-year-old – 1979			45–80	90	100–140	140–170	160–200
Macallan Gran Reserva – 18-year-old – 1980							170
Macallan Gran Reserva – 1981					105		
Macallan – 20-year-old – 1973 (First Cask)		70				65	
Macallan – 20-year-old – 1973 (Signatory, 53.5%)						45–65	
Macallan – 20-year-old – 1975 (First Cask)			33		37		50
Macallan – 24-year-old – 1975 (Douglas Laing, 50%)							45
Macallan – 25-year-old (Undated)	60	130–160	50–80				230
Macallan – 25-year-old (G & M Silver Jubilee)	110	120		145			
Macallan – 25-year-old (Magnum)		1000–1200					1400

Left to right.
Macallan – 1962,
Macallan-Glenlivet – 1937 (G & M),
Macallan – 37-year-old – 1937

Whisky Auction Sale Results (£s)	2000	2001	2002	2003	2004	2005	2006
Macallan – Glenlivet – 25-year-old – 1949	180–340	300					
Macallan – Glenlivet – 25-year-old – 1950	250		250				
Macallan – Glenlivet – 25-year-old – 1952	330	240–260					
Macallan – 25-year-old – 1957	260	190–360		320		230	550
Macallan – 25-year-old – 1958	125–250	150		220			300
Macallan – 25-year-old – 1962	90–175	140–160	100–115		160–190	190	190–260
Macallan – 25-year-old – 1962 (Crystal decanter)	170–180		220				
Macallan – 25-year-old – 1963 (Crystal decanter)			180–220	260	260		
Macallan – 25-year-old – 1964 (Crystal decanter)							480
Macallan – 25-year-old – 1963		300	140		260	190	220
Macallan – 25-year-old – 1964	70–160	130			210	220	190–200
Macallan – 25-year-old – 1965	170		110–140		150–210	160	
Macallan – 25-year-old – 1966		100			190	190	
Macallan – 25-year-old – 1967		130	170				190
Macallan – 25-year-old – 1968	80–140	90–110		160	160–210		210
Macallan – 25-year-old – 1969	110					200	
Macallan – 25-year-old – 1970				130			210
Macallan – 25-year-old – 1971				160	160	140–170	
Macallan – 25-year-old – 1971 (Milroy's)						80	
Macallan – 25-year-old – 1972	65		60–70	170	120	170	250
Macallan – 25-year-old – 1974				160			
Macallan – 25-year-old – 1973 (Murray McDavid)					30		
Macallan – 25-year-old – 1972 (Milroy's)			75				
Macallan – 26-year-old – 1968 (Signatory, 49%)			72		95	65–80	
Macallan – 28-year-old – 1965 (Signatory, 55.7%)							115

Whisky Auction Sale Results (£s)	2000	2001	2002	2003	2004	2005	2006
Macallan – 29-year-old – 1965 (First Cask)	300	100					
Macallan – 29-year-old – 1965 (Signatory)				100	70		
Macallan – 30-year-old	100			125	140–150		
Macallan – 30-year-old – 1963 (Cadenhead's, 54.7%)					105–130		140
Macallan – Glenlivet – 30-year-old – 1966 (Signatory)		100		100	60–200		
Macallan – 32-year-old – 1970 (54.9%)			400				
Macallan – 34-year-old – 1966 (Signatory, 51.2%)						90	
Macallan – 34-year-old – 1968 (Celtic Heartlands, 40.2%)							150–180
Macallan – Glenlivet – 35-year-old		250					
Macallan – 35-year-old – 1965 (Signatory)		90–110					
Macallan – 34-year-old – 1968 (Hart Bros, 43.1%)						55	
Macallan – 35-year-old – 1966 (Hart Bros, 41.9%)		80	40	53		55	
Macallan – 35-year-old – 1967 (Hart Bros, 41.9%)						50	
Macallan – 1978 (Speymalt, G & M)				30			33
Macallan – 1980 (59.3%)				90		100–110	
Macallan – 1980 (SMWS, 64.7%)						50	
Macallan – 1981 (59.3%)				53–60			
Macallan – 1981 (56%)						210	
Macallan Gran Reserva – 1981 (40%)					130		270
Macallan Fino Sherry – 1981		220		90			
Macallan – 1986 (SMWS, 57.7%)		50					
Macallan – 1989 (59.2%)						100	
Macallan – 1990 (57.4%)						58	
Macallan Elegancia – 1990					76		45

Macduff

These examples of Macduff listed are the only ones that have appeared at auction so far

Whisky Auction Sale Results (£s)	2000	2001	2002	2003	2004	2005	2006
Macduff – 8-year-old (Glen Deveron)				72			
Macduff – 11-year-old – 1975 (G & M)						75	90
Macduff – 12-year-old (Glen Deveron)					55		
MacDuff – 13-year-old – 1964 (Cadenhead's)			45–110				
MacDuff – 14-year-old – 1965 (Cadenhead's)					55		
Macduff – 18-year-old – 1963 (G & M)			85				
Macduff – 19-year-old – 1963 (G & M)			60				
Macduff – 1973 (SMWS, 58.3%)						40	
Macduff – 23-year-old – 1974 (Hart Bros, 43%)						20–30	
Macduff – 1975 (G & M)			25–37	45–72	35	25	31
Macduff – 28-year-old – 1965 (43.2%)						30	
Macduff – 28-year-old – 1973 (First Cask)					50–52		
Macduff – 31-year-old – 1972 (First Cask)					50		
MacDuff – 32-year-old – 1965 (Cadenhead's, 53%)				70	80		
Macduff – 36-year-old – 1965 (Douglas Laing, 49.2%)						100	70

Mannochmore

The Mannochmore Manager's Dram has proved to be very popular at auction

Whisky Auction Sale Results (£s)	2000	2001	2002	2003	2004	2005	2006
Loch Dhu – 10-year-old			40–45	37–65	62–120	48–85	62–100
Mannochmore – 12-year-old (Flora & Fauna)	38		20–35	40	27–40		20–50
Mannochmore – 18-year-old (Manager's Dram)	175	85–110	60–120	40–100	45–70	35–75	82–100
Mannochmore – 22-year-old – 1974 (60.1%)	36–47		30			42	57–70
Mannochmore – 22-year-old – 1977 (First Cask)					28	23	
Mannochmore – 1984 (G & M)				20			

Macduff – 13-year-old
(Cadenhead's)

Millburn

Only a small and varied selection of Millburn has made an appearance at auction, the Rare Malts have had the most exposure

Whisky Auction Sale Results (£s)	2000	2001	2002	2003	2004	2005	2006
Millburn – 12-year-old (James MacArthur)					20		
Millburn – 13-year-old – 1983 (Cadenhead's, 58.8%)					50		
Millburn – 16-year-old – 1966 (G & M)	57					95	
Millburn – 17-year-old – 1971 (G & M)						100	130
Millburn – 18-year-old – 1975 (58.9%)		43–57	60		37–62		50–65
Millburn – 18-year-old – 1983 (Signatory, 46%)					32		
Millburn – 20-year-old – 1966 (Crystal decanter)		300					
Millburn – 20-year-old – 1966 (Italian import)					210		
Millburn – 20-year-old – 1966 (G & M)							110
Millburn – 22-year-old – 1974 (59.8%)						60	
Millburn – 25-year-old – 1974 (Blackadder, 58.5%)				30			
Millburn – 25-year-old – 1975 (61.9%)					57		
Millburn – 25-year-old – 1975 (Douglas Laing, 58.9%)					60		
Millburn – 25-year-old – 1976 (Douglas Laing, 58.9%)							100
Millburn – 1971 (G & M)			32	47	31–42		27
Millburn – 1972 (G & M)					38		
Millburn – 1974 (G & M)							22
Millburn – 1979 (SMWS, 62.3%)							60

Milton Duff

Only a small selection of Milton Duff has made an appearance at auction recently

Whisky Auction Sale Results (£s)	2000	2001	2002	2003	2004	2005	2006
Milton Duff – Glenlivet – 5-year-old (Italian import)		80					
Milton Duff – 12-year-old (75 cl.)			20–50	33–53	38–53	40–92	20–27
Milton Duff – 13-year-old (26 2/3 f. oz, stopper cork)	75–85				230–250	220	330
Milton Duff – 15-year-old (Allied)				32		18–27	
Milton Duff – 20-year-old (Forth Wines, 95.5 degrees)					90		
Milton Duff – 21-year-old – 1963 (G & M)				80–100			
Milton Duff – 22-year-old (Crystal decanter)	250						
Milton Duff – 22-year-old – 1966 (Italian import)		100					
Milton Duff – 22-year-old – 1982 (First Cask)							39
Milton Duff – 23-year-old – 1973 (Hart Bros)					37	30	25
Milton Duff – 30-year-old – 1964 (Cadenhead's, 50.9%)					65–70		
Milton Duff – 35-year-old – 1964 (Italian import, 49.5%)	130						
Milton Duff – 35-year-old – 1966 (Douglas Laing, 41.1%)					55	45–50	50–52
Milton Duff – 1979 (G & M)						25	

Mortlach

Mature Mortlach bottled by Gordon & MacPhail has proved the most popular of the wide range that have appeared at auction to date

Whisky Auction Sale Results (£s)	2000	2001	2002	2003	2004	2005	2006
Mortlach Royal Wedding						70	
Mortlach – 10-year-old (Scottish Wildlife)			42				27
Mortlach – 10-year-old (Editor's Nose, 60.5%)			110	210		145	
Mortlach – Glenlivet – 10-year-old (Wine Society)				47			
Mortlach – 10-year-old – 1988 (Ian MacLeod, 43%)							55
Mortlach – 12-year-old (G & M, 75 cl.)	60–70		33–80	80–100		65–170	75
Mortlach – 12-year-old – 1988 (Signatory, 43%)							30
Mortlach – 13-year-old – 1984 (Signatory, 43%)					32		
Mortlach – 13-year-old – 1991 (Douglas Laing, 50%)					32		
Mortlach – 16-year-old (Flora & Fauna)	38		32–33	32	32	48	33–50
Mortlach – 19-year-old (Manager's Dram)					77–100	80–100	77–95
Mortlach – 19-year-old – 1980 (Adelphi, 59.3%)						32	22
Mortlach – 19-year-old – 1975 (Malt Master, 59.9%)						40	
Mortlach – 20-year-old – 1978 (62.2%)		53	36–40			75	62–72
Mortlach – 21-year-old – 1957 (Cadenhead's)			70				160
Mortlach – 22-year-old – 1957 (Cadenhead's)	110						180
Mortlach – 22-year-old – 1962 (Cadenhead's)	60						
Mortlach – 23-year-old – 1972 (59.4%)	36	46–65	40	40		65–77	90
Mortlach – 25-year-old (G & M, 75 cl.)		45	45	35			
Mortlach – 25-year-old – 1957 (Cadenhead's)			170				
Mortlach – 32-year-old (G Strachan)	200						

Whisky Auction Sale Results (£s)	2000	2001	2002	2003	2004	2005	2006
Mortlach – 32-year-old – 1962 (Cadenhead's, 42.8%)					90		
Mortlach – 32-year-old – 1971 (50.1%)							130
Mortlach – 35-year-old – 1936 (G & M)	180						
Mortlach – 36-year-old – 1936 (G & M)	190–235						
Mortlach – 39-year-old (G Strachan)	210	170		140		170	120
Mortlach – 43-year-old – 1936 (G & M)	260	300			230		250
Mortlach – 44-year-old – 1938 (G & M)					190		360
Mortlach – 1938 (G & M)	145–260	260				210	
Mortlach – 46-year-old – 1936 (G & M)					255	260	
Mortlach – 50-year-old – 1936 (G & M)			280				
Mortlach – 50-year-old – 1936 (Glass decanter, G & M)	350	360–520	400	350	220–360	220	440
Mortlach – 50-year-old – 1939 (Glass decanter, G & M)		325					
Mortlach – 1959 (G & M)					130		
Mortlach – 1960 (G & M)					75		

Mortlach – 25-year-old (G & M)

Mosstowie

Only a small selection of Mosstowie has made an appearance at auction in recent years

Whisky Auction Sale Results (£s)	2000	2001	2002	2003	2004	2005	2006
Mosstowie – 15-year-old (Crystal decanter)	290						
Mosstowie – 17-year-old (Crystal decanter)		320					
Mosstowie – 12-year-old – 1970 (G & M)			37			90	
Mosstowie – 1970 (G & M)	60		60				
Mosstowie – 1975 (G & M)		38	26–40		23–40	39	
Mosstowie – 21-year-old – 1976 (Silent Stills, 54.8%)	52		65				
Mosstowie – 1979 (G & M)						24–39	30

North British

Only a small selection of Single Grain whisky from North British has made an appearance at auction so far the highest price paid for a rare distillery bottling

Whisky Auction Sale Results (£s)	2000	2001	2002	2003	2004	2005	2006
North British – 1964 (Signatory, 46%)	42–90						
North British – 1980 (60.3%)						58	
North British – 1980 (61.5%)	35						50
North British – 15-year-old – 1979 (Signatory, 43%)					37		
North British – 18-year-old – 1979 (Signatory, 43%)					20		
North British – 21-year-old (Cadenhead's, 57.8%)							35
North British – 25-year-old – 1964 (Signatory, 46%)		43					
North British – 40-year-old (Distillery, 1000 bottles, 57.4%)				300			

North Port
(Cadenhead's)

North Port

Only a small selection of North Port has made an appearance at auction to date

Whisky Auction Sale Results (£s)	2000	2001	2002	2003	2004	2005	2006
North Port – 14-year-old – 1968 (G & M)					80	90–105	
North Port – 15-year-old – 1964 (Cadenhead's, 45.7%)			90			100	130
North Port – 17-year-old – 1964 (Cadenhead's, 46%)			70				
North Port – 17-year-old – 1970 (G & M)					80–90		110
North Port – Brechin – 1970 (G & M)			20–71		23–40	77	
North Port – Brechin – 1974 (G & M)	26–46		26	21–30	33		
North Port – Brechin – 18-year-old – 1976 (Cadenhead's, 61.4%)							45
North Port – 1977 (SMWS, 62.4%)							85
North Port – 20-year-old – 1979 (61.2%)		43	42		70	30	65–75
North Port Brechin – 23-year-old – 1976 (Dormant Distillery, 60.4%)					45		
North Port – Brechin – 1981 (G & M)							32
North Port – 23-year-old – 1971 (54.7%)						110	
North Port Brechin – 24-year-old – 1976 (Adelphi, 60.4%)					45		
North Port Brechin – 24-year-old – 1976 (First Cask, 46%)					36		39
North Port Brechin – 33-year-old – 1970 (Douglas Laing, 49.7%)							80
North Port – 36-year-old – 1966 (Douglas Laing, 50%)				60	70–100		60

Oban

Of all the Manager's Drams, Oban has the largest selection, they have proved to be very popular at auction, the 200th Anniversary bottling particularly

Whisky Auction Sale Results (£s)	2000	2001	2002	2003	2004	2005	2006
Oban – 12-year-old (J Hopkins & Co)		80	55–100	97–102	40–80	75–130	110–230
Oban – 13-year-old (Manager's Dram)	153–216	100–112	60–300	100–160	190	110–235	176
Oban – 14-year-old (Classic Malts, 200th Anniversary)		80	33		50	33	40
Oban – 14-year-old – 1972 (G & M)				130			
Oban – 19-year-old (Manager's Dram)	130–180	110–210	53–127	70–110	75–105	110–250	80–145
Oban – 19-year-old							
(Manager's Dram, low spirit level)							65
Oban – 16-year-old							
(Manager's Dram, 200th Anniversary)	280–330	95–220	113–210	150–210	175–200	150–230	190–230
Oban – 30-year-old – 1963 (Cadenhead's, 52%)					160		135
Oban – 32-year-old – 1969 (55.1%)						120–160	130
Oban – 1972 (G & M)					32		
Oban – 1980 (Double matured)			27			35	30
Oban – 1990 (Double matured)							25
Oban – 1991 (Double matured)							32

Ord

These expressions of Ord include a rare early 20th century example, the very popular Manager's Drams and the Maltings 25th Anniversary bottling

Whisky Auction Sale Results (£s)	2000	2001	2002	2003	2004	2005	2006
Ord – Bottled 1923 (J Dewar & Sons)			2200				
Ord – Over – 5-year-old (P Dawson Ltd)		140					
Ord – 12-year-old (P Dawson Ltd, 26 2/3 fl. oz)			50–95		85	125	
Glenordie – 12-year-old (J Dewar & Sons, 75 cl.)				45	75	37–125	
Ord – 16-year-old (Manager's Dram)	153–280	140	60–120	50–135	75–105	135–155	120–135
Ord – 20-year-old – 1962 (Cadenhead's, 46%)					120		150
Glen Ord – 23-year-old – 1973 (59.8%)			37			45	47–65
Glen Ord – 23-year-old – 1974 (60.8%)					27		
Glen Ord – 25-year-old (58.3%)							70
Glen Ord – 28-year-old (58.3%)							90
Ord – 31-year-old – 1962 (Cadenhead's, 53%)		70–160		60	120		
Ord – 1962 (R W Duthie, 58%)	155						
Glen Ord Maltings – 25th Anniversary – 1969			260–280	160–200	190–230		320

Glen Ord Maltings –
25 Anniversary

Parkmore

These rare examples of Parkmore were the first to appear at auction after the Millennium, in 2001

Whisky Auction Sale Results (£s)	2000	2001	2002	2003	2004	2005	2006
Parkmore – 16-year-old – 1911		2700					
Parkmore Fine Old Scotch Whisky – 7-year-old – Late 19th century		2100					

Parkmore – 1911

Pittyvaich

Independent, the Flora & Fauna bottling and Scotch Malt Whisky Society expression of Pittyvaich have been sold with success at auction recently

Whisky Auction Sale Results (£s)	2000	2001	2002	2003	2004	2005	2006
Pittyvaich – 12-year-old (Flora & Fauna)	38	30	27–32	36	32–35		20–53
Pittyvaich – 12-year-old (J MacArthur, 55%)			23		30	18	
Pittyvaich – 12-year-old (J MacArthur, 53.5%)							55
Pittyvaich – Glenlivet – 13-year-old – 1977 (Cadenhead's, 58.4%)					105		
Pittyvaich – 14-year-old (J MacArthur, 54.5%)			37		115		
Pittyvaich – 1976 (SMWS, 57.2%)			147				
Pittyvaich – 1977 (Cadenhead's, 56.6%)				80			
Pittyvaich – 1977 (Cadenhead's, 55.8%)					70		

Pittyvaich Flora &
Fauna – 12-year-old

Port Ellen

To date, Port Ellen holds the 5th highest record price for the sale of a bottle of single malt whisky at auction that fetched £11,000, in April 2001, the Maltings 25th Anniversary bottling is quite sought after

Whisky Auction Sale Results (£s)	2000	2001	2002	2003	2004	2005	2006
Port Ellen – 1891 (John Ramsay Distillers)		11,000					
Port Ellen – 15-year-old – 1882 (J Murray & Sons)			3800				
Port Ellen Maltings – 25th Anniversary (58.4%)	520–610	600–650	560–570	570–680	520–550	780	1000–1300
Port Ellen – 10-year-old (Scottish Wildlife)						90	
Port Ellen – 11-year-old – 1983 (Italian import, 43%)				70			
Port Ellen – 12-year-old (Scottish Wildlife)			42				
Port Ellen – 12-year-old (D Murdoch & Co)			90–180	70			110
Port Ellen – 13-year-old – 1979 (D Murdoch & Co)		60					
Port Ellen – 14-year-old – 1983 (Coopers' Choice, 55.8%)		160		45			
Port Ellen – 15-year-old – 1979 (Signatory. 43%)						60	
Port Ellen – 16-year-old – 1983 (Coopers' Choice, 55.9%)		160					
Port Ellen – 16-year-old – 1969 (G & M)		320–380	120–270		320	210	
Port Ellen – 16-year-old – 1970 (G & M)					230–300		255
Port Ellen – 16-year-old – 1977 (G & M)						100	
Port Ellen – 16-year-old – 1977 (Italian import)	170						
Port Ellen – 16-year-old – 1977 (Wilson & Morgan)	140						
Port Ellen – 16-year-old – 1980 (First Cask)		140			140–175	110	
Port Ellen – 16-year-old – 1980 (Cadenhead's, 63%)				45			
Port Ellen – 16-year-old – 1983 (Coopers' Choice, 43%)			60				

Whisky Auction Sale Results (£s)	2000	2001	2002	2003	2004	2005	2006
Port Ellen – 17-year-old (D Murdoch & Co, 59.5%)					155		
Port Ellen – 17-year-old – 1981 (46%)			60				
Port Ellen – 17-year-old – 1970 (G & M)			320				
Port Ellen – 18-year-old – 1981 (D McGibbon, 43%)				37		40	
Port Ellen – 18-year-old – 1976 (First Cask)		165–190			140–165	220	150
Port Ellen – 18-year-old – 1977 (Wilson & Morgan)	140						
Port Ellen – 18-year-old – 1979 (Silent Stills, 56.3%)			90				
Port Ellen – 18-year-old – 1981 (Old Malt Cask, 50%)			50	30			
Port Ellen – 18-year-old – 1982 (Old Malt Cask, 50%)						45	
Port Ellen – 19-year-old – 1970 (Italian import)	370	220					
Port Ellen – 19-year-old – 1976 (Hart Bros, 43%)			60				
Port Ellen – 19-year-old – 1981 (The Bottlers, 60.4%)							120
Port Ellen – 19-year-old – 1982 (Douglas Laing, 50%)					50		60
Port Ellen – 20-year-old – 1978 (60.9%)	55		57	35–45	55–80	55–175	
Port Ellen – 20-year-old – 1982 (Douglas Laing, 50%)					40		50
Port Ellen – 21-year-old – 1976 (Wilson & Morgan)	140						
Port Ellen – 21-year-old – 1976 (Signatory, 57.9%)						60	
Port Ellen – 21-year-old – 1979 (Douglas Laing, 50%)				30		50	
Port Ellen – 21-year-old – 1980 (Silver Seal, 43%)						70	
Port Ellen – 21-year-old – 1982 (Douglas Laing, 50%)						45–50	35
Port Ellen – 23-year-old (Italian import, 45%)			190				
Port Ellen – 22-year-old – 1976 (Signatory. 56.2%)						50–60	
Port Ellen – 22-year-old – 1978 (60.5%)						45–100	60–65
Port Ellen – 22-year-old – 1979 (56.2%)				100	60–95	87–105	110–135
Port Ellen – 22-year-old – 1979 (Signatory, 43%)							90

Whisky Auction Sale Results (&s)	2000	2001	2002	2003	2004	2005	2006
Port Ellen – 23-year-old – 1975 (Italian import, 45%)	110						
Port Ellen – 23-year-old – 1975 (Signatory, 43%)				60			75
Port Ellen – 23-year-old – 1978 (Signatory, 58.1%)				95			100
Port Ellen – 23-year-old – 1978 (Signatory, 59%)							100
Port Ellen – 23-year-old – 1978 (Douglas Laing, 50%)					50		50
Port Ellen – 23-year-old – 1979 (Signatory, 43%)					65		35
Port Ellen – 24-year-old – 1978 (59.35%)					77–95	55–70	90
Port Ellen – 24-year-old – 1978 (57.9%)					60–90	80	90
Port Ellen – 24-year-old – 1975 (Prestonfield House, 46%)			95				

Port Ellen Maltings –
21-year-old

Whisky Auction Sale Results (£s)	2000	2001	2002	2003	2004	2005	2006
Port Ellen – 24-year-old – 1975 (Adelphi, 56%)							60
Port Ellen – 24-year-old – 1976 (Douglas Laing, 50%)				30			
Port Ellen – 25-year-old – 1976 (Douglas Laing, 50%)					90		60
Port Ellen – 25-year-old – 1978 (Douglas Laing, 50%)						50	
Port Ellen – 25-year-old – 1978 (56.2%)							90
Port Ellen – 31-year-old – 1969 (Silver Seal, 40%)				170–190			
Port Ellen – 1970 (G & M)	58		72–78		75		
Port Ellen – 1970 (12 miniatures, G & M)			60–80				
Port Ellen – 1970 (G & M)				90			
Port Ellen – 1971 (G & M)						77	
Port Ellen – 1974 (G & M)					67–85		
Port Ellen – 1977 (Scott's Selection, 52.5%)		60		45			
Port Ellen – 1979 (G & M, 61.1%)		80					
Port Ellen – 1979 (G & M, 60.7%)							60–77
Port Ellen – 1979 (G & M, 40%)					33		
Port Ellen – 1980 (G & M)	28			33–37	30	25–80	25
Port Ellen – 1980 (G & M, 64.7%)						53	
Port Ellen – 1980 (G & M, 63.9%)							55
Port Ellen – 1981 (G & M)		37		37	42	30–40	60
Port Ellen – 1982 (G & M)							37–52
Port Ellen – 1983 (Italian import, 50%)		105–130					
Port Ellen – 1983 (Scott's Selection, 55.5%)					65		

Pulteney

From Pulteney distillery, there have been only a handful of expressions of bottles sold recently at auction

Whisky Auction Sale Results (£s)	2000	2001	2002	2003	2004	2005	2006
Old Pulteney (26 2/3 fl. oz)		380					
Old Pulteney – 8-year-old (G & M)			65–66		30–53		
Old Pulteney – 15-year-old (G & M, 75 cl.)					40	70	
Old Pulteney – 15-year-old (60.6%)		35				52	47–50
Old Pulteney – 15-year-old (60.5%)						52	
Old Pulteney Millennium – 15-year-old (60.9%)		35–45					
Old Pulteney Millennium – 15-year-old (59.8%)			33		40		40
Old Pulteney – 1961 (G & M)	90	50	25	45	75–80		80–90
Old Pulteney – 18-year-old (Cask 1303, 58.4%)							47
Pulteney – 18-year-old – 1974 (Signatory, 59.1%)		43					
Pulteney – 19-year-old – 1984 (Adelphi, 51.9%)							20
Pulteney – 19-year-old – 1974 (First Cask)		30			25		
Old Pulteney – 20-year-old – 1968 (Italian import)		90					
Old Pulteney – 26-year-old (46%)							30
Pulteney – 34-year-old – 1967 (Douglas laing, 54.9%)							70
Pulteney – 36-year-old – 1964 (Douglas Laing, 50%)						55	80
Old Pulteney – 1983 (58.4%)							47–50

Rieclachan

This rare expression is the only historical bottling from Rieclachan distillery that has been sold at auction over the last decade

Whisky Auction Sale Results (£s)	2000	2001	2002	2003	2004	2005	2006
Rieclachan – 10-year-old – Believed early 20th century (Wylie, Mitchell & Co)		3600					

Left to right.
Old Pultney – 1983,
Old Pultney – 18-year-old,
Old Pultney – 15-year-old,
Old Pultney – 1961

Rosebank

Rosebank makes a rare appearance at auction and older bottlings are sure to attract great interest

Whisky Auction Sale Results (£s)	2000	2001	2002	2003	2004	2005	2006
Rosebank – 1906 (Matthew Gloag & Son)	1200						
Rosebank – 1938 (R Stewart & Son)				300			
Rosebank (Distillers Agency)			150–250		150		260
Rosebank – 7-year-old – 1989 (Signatory, 43%)						25	
Rosebank – 8-year-old (Bristol Brandy Co, 43%)				40–47	28		
Rosebank – 8-year-old (Distillers Agency)	60		44–140	220	80–210	140–190	190
Rosebank – 8-year-old – 1989 (Cadenhead's, 57.9%)					50	25	37
Rosebank – 8-year-old – 1990 (Signatory, 43%)				45			
Rosebank – 8-year-old – 1990 (Murray McDavid, 46%)						30	
Rosebank – 9-year-old – 1990 (Signatory, 46%)				45		25–40	
Rosebank – 10-year-old – 1989 (Cadenhead's, 58.6%)						39	
Rosebank – 10-year-old – 1989 (Silent Stills, 56.2%)						140	
Rosebank – 10-year-old – 1992 (D McGibbon, 46%)							30
Rosebank – 11-year-old – 1980 (Cadenhead's, 60.1%)						42	
Rosebank – 11-year-old – 1989 (D McGibbon, 43%)							30
Rosebank – 11-year-old – 1989 (Murray McDavid, 46%)						30	
Rosebank – 11-year-old – 1989 (Cadenhead's, 46%)						39	
Rosebank – 11-year-old – 1989 (Douglas Laing, 50%)							37
Rosebank – 11-year-old – 1989 (Cadenhead's, 59%)						34	
Rosebank – 11-year-old – 1991 (Ian MacLeod, 43%)							27
Rosebank – 12-year-old – 1989 (Cadenhead's, 58.6%)						34	

Whisky Auction Sale Results (£s)	2000	2001	2002	2003	2004	2005	2006
Rosebank – 12-year-old (Flora & Fauna)	38		20–35	36–48	32–50	33–44	25–53
Rosebank – 12-year-old (Distillers Agency)	270	70–150			70–105	100	
Rosebank – 13-year-old – 1980 (Cadenhead's, 59.3%)				40		42	
Rosebank – 13-year-old – 1990 (Hart Bros, 58.3%)							27
Rosebank – 15-year-old (Distillers Agency, Italian import, 61%)	110–160						
Rosebank – 15-year-old (Distillers Agency, Italian import, 50%)	45–150	110–130	115				
Rosebank – 16-year-old – 1989 (Mission Selection 5, 46%)							38
Rosebank – 17-year-old – 1974 (Signatory, 43%)					37–50	45	
Rosebank – 18-year-old – 1974 (Signaotry, 43%)					43	25	30
Rosebank – 20-year-old (Distillers Agency, Italian import, 57%)	160	120–200	180			150–180	

Left to right.
Rosebank – 8-year-old,
Rosebank (Distillers Agency),
Rosebank – 8-year-old

Whisky Auction Sale Results (£s)	2000	2001	2002	2003	2004	2005	2006
Rosebank – 20-year-old (G Strachan)	280						
Rosebank – 20-year-old – 1979 (60.3%)		43				40	75–100
Rosebank – 20-year-old – 1981 (63.8%)							60
Rosebank – 25-year-old – 1967 (Signatory, 54.4%)						110	
Rosebank – 26-year-old – 1967 (Signatory, 51.7%)					110		
Rosebank – 26-year-old – 1967 (Signatory, 54.4%)					110		
Rosebank – 28-year-old – 1965 (Signatory, 53.4%)					100	120	
Rosebank – 34-year-old (G Strachan)	80		200	130		180	
Rosebank – 1976 (SMWS, 57.3%)					210		
Rosebank – 1979 (G & M)				20–30		47	27
Rosebank – 1979 (SMWS, 58.5%)							70
Rosebank – 1981 (63.9%)	23	45	40			80	50–75
Rosebank – 1983 (G & M)					40	40	
Rosebank – 1984 (G & M)				30		40	50
Rosebank – 1985 (SMWS, 56.5%)				30			70
Rosebank – 1988 (G & M)						27	
Rosebank – 1989 (G & M)			37		27		27
Rosebank – 1989 (SMWS, 59.8%)						40	
Rosebank – 1989 (SMWS, 58.9%)							33
Rosebank – 1989 (SMWS, 59.4%)							33
Rosebank – 1989 (SMWS, 59.1%)							33
Rosebank – 1989 (German import, 60.6%)				50			
Rosebank – 1992 (SMWS, 59.4%)						100	
Rosebank – 1992 (SMWS, 59.4%)					70–105		

Royal Brackla

The Royal Brackla – 60-year-old represents excellent value for such a rare and mature single malt

Whisky Auction Sale Results (£s)	2000	2001	2002	2003	2004	2005	2006
Brackla – 1897 (Matthew Gloag & Son)	1500						
Royal Brackla – 12-year-old (Italian import, 43%)	42–48						
Royal Brackla – 10-year-old (Flora & Fauna)			36		27		25–52
Royal Brackla – 10-year-old – 1969 (G & M, 70 degrees)							100
Royal Brackla – 12-year-old (James MacArthur, 65%)			27				
Royal Brackla – 14-year-old – 1978 (Master of Malt, 43%)					38		
Royal Brackla – 14-year-old – 1969 (G & M)						100	
Royal Brackla – 16-year-old (Italian import, 57%)	42–48						
Royal Brackla – 16-year-old – 1970 (G & M)	58						
Royal Brackla – 18-year-old – 1979 (Hart Bros, 43%)						20–24	
Royal Brackla – 1970 (G & M)			35		40		
Royal Brackla – 1972 (G & M)		50			36–40	38	
Royal Brackla – 20-year-old – 1978 (59.8%)		35			35–52		47
Royal Brackla – 22-year-old – 1976 (Douglas Laing, 50%)							45
Royal Brackla – 25-year-old – 1978 (43%)					100		
Royal Brackla – 27-year-old – 1975 (Mission, Ser. 1, 46%)							30–40
Royal Brackla – 1979 (McDowall, 43%)						40	25–27

Whisky Auction Sale Results (£s)	2000	2001	2002	2003	2004	2005	2006
Royal Brackla – 60-year-old – 1924 (Accompanied by miniature)	1950	1500–1700	1300–1850	850	1200	1000–1250	1200–1500
Royal Brackla – 60-year-old – 1924	1800–1900				1100		

Royal Brackla –
60-year-old – 1924

Royal Lochnagar

Only a small selection of Royal Lochnagar has made an appearance at auction, the Selected Reserve and Rare Malts having had the most exposure, the 150th Anniversary bottling is quite sought after

Whisky Auction Sale Results (£s)	2000	2001	2002	2003	2004	2005	2006
Royal Lochnagar – 12-year-old (150th Anniversary, 150 bottles)					420	400	
Lochnagar – 12-year-old (John Begg)	60		53	30–47	35–55	85	80
Lochnagar – 1960 (Commemorative half bottle)	85–110						
Royal Lochnagar Selected Reserve	85	60–100	80	60–110	50–90	105	90–100
Royal Lochnagar Selected Reserve (Unboxed)	45					30	
Royal Lochnagar – 12-year-old (70 cl.)	25					85	21
Royal Lochnagar – 14-year-old – 1969 (G & M)					82		
Royal Lochnagar – 23-year-old – 1973 (59.7%)	47	47	47–83			30–60	
Royal Lochnagar – 24-year-old – 1972 (55.7%)	36			40	27–32	90	53–80
Royal Lochnagar – 27-year-old – 1952 (G & M)			170				170
Royal Lochnagar – 29-year-old – 1952 (G & M)			130				
Lochnagar – 30-year-old – 1972 (Douglas Laing, 50%)				95	50		
Lochnagar – 30-year-old – 1972 (Douglas Laing, 57.6%)						75–90	
Lochnagar – 30-year-old – 1973 (Douglas Laing, 57.9%)						65	
Lochnagar – 32-year-old – 1972 (Douglas Laing, 60.5%)					90		

Scapa

Only a small selection of Scapa has made an appearance at auction to date

Whisky Auction Sale Results (£s)	2000	2001	2002	2003	2004	2005	2006
Scapa – 8-year-old (G & M, 26 2/3 fl. oz)	50		67–73				
Scapa – 8-year-old (G & M, 75 cl.)					27–33		
Scapa – 10-year-old (Taylor & Ferguson)				102			30
Scapa – 15-year-old – 1965 (Cadenhead's, 46%)							100
Scapa – 16-year-old – 1980 (Barrel shaped, 43%)					32		
Scapa – 1963 (G & M)	60						
Scapa – 1965 (Italian import, 46%)			122				
Scapa – 1965 (Cadenhead's, 49.6%)			190				
Scapa – 1966 (G & M)				90			
Scapa – 1979 (SMWS, 62.4%)		189					
Scapa – 1979 (SMWS, 59.8%)						50	
Scapa – 1979 (G & M)					25	35	
Scapa – 1980 (SMWS, 58.8%)					70		
Scapa – 1983 (G & M)		38	25			32–35	
Scapa – 1985 (G & M)						32	
Scapa – 1986 (G & M)	25				30		

Singleton

Only a small selection of Singleton has made an appearance at auction to date, the distillery anniversary cask strength bottling fetching the most

Whisky Auction Sale Results (£s)	2000	2001	2002	2003	2004	2005	2006
Singleton of Auchroisk – 10-year-old (On stand, 75 cl.)					70		
Singleton of Auchroisk – 10-year-old – 1989 (Cadenhead's, 46%)							33
Singleton of Auchroisk – 10-year-old (Bottled for Craigendarroch Hotel, 1995)					150		
Singleton Anniversary – 20-year-old (59%)	650			780	360–620	500–550	450
Singleton of Auchroisk – 28-year-old – 1974 (56.8%)							68
Singleton of Auchroisk – 1975			40–50	43	34–76	33	55–77
Singleton of Auchroisk – 1976			41	23	32	47	47
Auchroisk – 1978 (SMWS, 58.3%)			55				
Singleton of Auchroisk – 1978	43	30					
Singleton Particular – 1978						85	
Singleton Particular – 1980	55				70	75	
Singleton of Auchroisk – 1981	30					47	27–50
Singleton of Auchroisk – 1983	18		60	20–23	30–43	50–90	

Speyburn

Only a small selection of Speyburn has made an appearance at auction so far

Whisky Auction Sale Results (£s)	2000	2001	2002	2003	2004	2005	2006
Speyburn – 12-year-old (Flora & Fauna)					32–40		37–53
Speyburn – Glenlivet – 12-year-old – 1967 (Cadenhead's, 45.7%)							70–115
Speyburn – 13-year-old – 1971 (G & M)					50		
Speyburn – 15-year-old – 1968 (G & M)						80	
Speyburn – 16-year-old – 1986 (46%)							23–47
Speyburn Centenary – 21-year-old		80				110	
Speyburn – 1967 (Italian import)		122					
Speyburn – 1971 (G & M)			20–60		23	26	32
Speyburn – 21-year-old – 1978 (58.8%)					35		
Speyburn – 27-year-old – 1973 (46%)				25	35		30

Speyburn Flora & Fauna – 12-year-old

Springbank

Green Springbank has risen immensely in value over the last decade, the distillery has produced a large range of spirits spanning many years and is among the most collected malts

Whisky Auction Sale Results (£s)	2000	2001	2002	2003	2004	2005	2006
Springbank – 50-year-old – 1919 (Pear shaped)	2000	3800		1600		1600	1350
Springbank New Release: 25, 30, 35, 40, 45, 50-year-old with set of miniatures			4200	1200–1900	1900	1700–2100	3000
Springbank New Release miniatures				350			
Springbank Ageing Monography (R W Duthie, Samaroli, 6 bottles)	490	500–550	450				
Springbank C.V.					40	40	48
Springbank – 5-year-old	120						
Springbank – 5-year-old (Magnum)	260	220					
Springbank – 5-year-old – 1993 (Adelphi, 61.2%)				50			
Springbank Da Mhille Organic – 7-year-old	190	90			90–100	110	100
Springbank Da Mhille Organic – 7-year-old (Bottle number 2 of 100)	400						
Springbank – 8-year-old	87	220					
Springbank – 8-year-old (Ceramic book, 43%)						90	
Springbank (Glen's Extra – 8-year-old)		140					
Springbank Ceramic Library, 75cl: (8, 10, 12, 15-year-olds)	300–400						
Springbank Ceramic Library, 70cl: (8, 10, 12, 15-year-olds)		250–270					330
Springbank – 10-year-old (26 2/3 fl. oz)					340		

The Whiskymouse

Whiskies - Spirits - Liqueurs

www.whiskymouse.com

Telephone: 07730 059011

Whisky Auction Sale Results (£s)	2000	2001	2002	2003	2004	2005	2006
Springbank – 10-year-old (75 cl.)			65				
Springbank – 10-year-old (Pear shaped, 26 2/3 fl. oz, 70 degrees)			125				
Springbank – 10-year-old (Ceramic jug, 26 2/3 fl. ozs.)						70	
Springbank – 10-year-old (Isle of Gigha, 200 bottles, 46%)			220–360		320–340		200
Springbank – 10-year-old – 1967 (Sherry butt No. 3129, 59%)	220						
Springbank – 10-year-old – 1973 (Sherry cask matured, 57%)	390						
Springbank – 12-year-old (Samaroli import, 57.1%)	200						

Left to right.
Green Springbank –
18-year-old-1973,
Springbank Spirit of Gigha –
10-year-old

Whisky Auction Sale Results (£s)	2000	2001	2002	2003	2004	2005	2006
Springbank (Glen's Extra – 12-year-old)		190					
Springbank – 12-year-old (26 2/3 fl. oz, 80 degrees)				220	230–440		120–190
Springbank – 12-year-old (75 cl.)		220	65–125	60	90–200	110	130
Springbank – 12-year-old (Cadenhead's)						380	
Springbank – 12-year-old (Ceramic jug)			40	95	60–70	120	90–120
Springbank Bond Reserve – 12-year-old (Cadenhead's, 51.6%)							55
Springbank – 12-year-old (Distillery Walk from Fettercairn, 2003, 50.2%)					1250		
Springbank – 12-year-old – 175th Anniversary					85	40–45	40–55
Springbank Rum Wood – 12-year-old – 1989 (54.6%)				40–57	60–80	37–60	50–55
Springbank Bourbon Wood – 12-year-old – 1991 (58.5%)						35–52	40–50

Left to right.
Springbank Distillery Walk From Fettercairn,
Springbank – 12-year-old

Whisky Auction Sale Results (£s)	2000	2001	2002	2003	2004	2005	2006
Springbank Port Wood – 13-year-old – 1989 (54.2%)						45–58	37–57
Springbank – 13-year-old – 1989 (Cadenhead's, 56.1%)						30	
Springbank Port Wood – 14-year-old – 1989 (52.8%)							37
Springbank – 15-year-old (75 cl.)	82	200–220	65–110	125–135	93–150	55–57	50
Springbank – 15-year-old (Pear shaped)	190–270	140					
Springbank – 15-year-old – 1979			125				
Springbank – 15-year-old (European Summit, 1992)		170					
Springbank – 15-year-old (The MacLennan Malt, 46%)			300				
Springbank – 15-year-old (Burnside for Eaglesome, 70 cl.)			85		82		
Springbank – 15-year-old (Ceramic jug)		235					
Springbank – 18-year-old – 1973 (Green, 57.5%)	310–320	520–590	460		550	500	450–480
Springbank – 18-year-old – 1973 (Green, 57.9%)		530–620	450–560		550–580	540–550	440–460
Springbank (Dell Fines – 20-year-old)	200						
Springbank – 1964 (Lateltin, 46%)						255	
Springbank (Prestonfield House) – 20-year-old – 1967		250					
Springbank – 20-year-old – 1967 (Signatory, Dun Dideann, 46%)						120	
Springbank – 20-year-old (Bottled 1999, last bottling of 20th century, 57 bottles)			580				750
Springbank – 21-year-old (Bottled 1999, last bottling of 20th century, 59 bottles)			580				750

Whisky Auction Sale Results (£s)	2000	2001	2002	2003	2004	2005	2006
Springbank – 21-year-old (26 2/3 fl. oz, stopper cork, 100 degrees)				500			
Springbank – 21-year-old (70 cl., dumpy)	82–120	135–210	100–180	135	70–110	120–195	160
Springbank – 21-year-old (70 cl., tall)				70–87	67–110	55–90	62–100
Springbank – 21-year-old (Pear shaped)	190–260	200					
Springbank – 22-year-old (Cadenhead's, 46%)			130			250	
Springbank – 22-year-old (Cadenhead's, 80 degrees)					360		
Springbank – 22-year-old – 1972 (46%)				190			
Springbank – 24-year-old – 1966 (Cask 442, 61.2%)	380					860	900
Springbank – 24-year-old – 1967 (46%)						220	
Springbank – 24-year-old – 1966 (Cask 443, 58.1%)		560					
Springbank – 24-year-old – 1966 (Cask 441, 60.7%)		680					
Springbank – 25-year-old (Half)						80	
Springbank – 25-year-old (70 cl., dumpy)	85–130	200		170	70–120	290	
Springbank – 25-year-old (Pear shaped)	210	220				290	260
Springbank – 25-year-old – 1953 (Cadenhead's, 45.7%)			200				
Springbank – 25-year-old – 1954 (Cadenhead's, 45.7%)							420
Springbank New Release – 25-year-old			115–170			180	
Springbank – 25-year-old (Frank McHardy)						250–260	200–300
Springbank – 26-year-old – 1965 (46%)						260	
Springbank – 26-year-old – 1969 (First Cask)		90			140		
Springbank – 26-year-old – 1969 (Signatory, 51.7%)				110			
Springbank – 26-year-old – 1965 (Milroy's, 46%)					180		
Springbank – 27-year-old – 1969 (Signatory, 54%)				120			

Whisky Auction Sale Results (£s)	2000	2001	2002	2003	2004	2005	2006
Springbank – 27-year-old – 1965 (Mary Quant label, Everest Challenge, 46%)			680–900				
Springbank – 27-year-old – 1974 (Ian MacLeod, 56.6%)					60–130		
Springbank – 28-year-old – 1969 (Murray McDavid, 46%)				120			
Springbank – 28-year-old – 1974 (Ian MacLeod, 46%)					70–100		100
Springbank – 29-year-old – 1962 (46%)				270–280	260		360
Springbank – 30-year-old – 1950 (Cadenhead's, 46%)					350		
Springbank – 30-year-old – 1972 (Ian MacLeod, 57.8%)					85–130		
Springbank – 30-year-old (Released 1999, 46%)			140	220			
Springbank – 30-year-old (Dumpy, 70 cl.)	95–120	100–110	210	140	130		
Springbank – 30-year-old (Milroy's)			100				
Springbank – 30-year-old – 1965 (Hart Bros)	50						
Springbank – 30-year-old – 1966 (Cask 1648, 46%)						240	
Springbank – 30-year-old – 1969 (Signatory)		80					
Springbank – 31-year-old – 1963 (Cadenhead's, 52.3%)			300		240		
Springbank – 31-year-old – 1967 (Murray McDavid, 46%)							120
Springbank – 32-year-old – 1964 (Adelphi, 50.8%)				140			
Springbank – 32-year-old – 1967 (Cadenhead's)		90					
Springbank – 32-year-old – 1966 (Cask 491, 56.9%)			220				
Springbank – 32-year-old (70 cl., 46%)							180–210
Springbank – 33-year-old (Pear shaped)	310	280				340–350	350
Springbank – 33-year-old – 1970 (Adelphi, 54.4%)						120–190	
Springbank – 34-year-old – 1964 (Cadenhead's, 52.2%)	240				320		210
Springbank – 34-year-old – 1965 (Murray McDavid, 46%)							170

Whisky Auction Sale Results (£s)	2000	2001	2002	2003	2004	2005	2006
Springbank – 34-year-old – 1965 (Douglas Laing, 40.9%)							100
Springbank – 34-year-old – 1966							
(Limited edition of 300, 47.1%)		380		260–340			
Springbank – 34-year-old – 1967 (Hart Bros, 40.9%)		70	62		62	50	
Springbank – 34-year-old – 1969 (Old Malt Cask)		80–100					
Springbank – 35-year-old (New release, 46%)			160				
Springbank – 50-year-old (New release, 40.5%)					550		800
Springbank (Campbeltown) – 1952 (45.5%)	850						
Springbank – 1963	260						
Springbank – 1964 (46%)						310–350	450
Springbank – 1964 (SMWS, 51%)		233					
Springbank – 1965 (46%)							360
Springbank – 1965 (SMWS, 57.9%)		233					
Springbank – 1965 (SMWS, 53%)		233					
Springbank – 1965 (Adelphi, 53.2%)					185		
Springbank – 1965 (Cadenhead's, 54.4%)					240		
Springbank Local Barley – 1965 (Cask 007, 50.4%)			180		240	270	300
Springbank Local Barley – 1965 (Cask 008, 47.6%)					220		
Springbank Local Barley – 1965 (Cask 009, 52.4%)					240	280	300–320
Springbank Local Barley – 1965 (Cask 010, 49.1%)					230		
Springbank – 1966 (46%)	410					270	
Springbank Local Barley – 1966 (Cask 475, 52%)							390
Springbank Local Barley – 1966 (Cask 473, 52.5%)							380
Springbank Local Barley – 1966 (Cask 476, 52%)					280		
Springbank Local Barley – 1966 (Cask 477, 53.6%)							440

Whisky Auction Sale Results (£s)	2000	2001	2002	2003	2004	2005	2006
Springbank Local Barley – 1966 (Cask 490, 54%)			150–160				
Springbank Local Barley – 1966 (Cask 492, 55.1%)						320	
Springbank Local Barley – 1966 (Cask 493, 56.8%)					260		
Springbank Local Barley – 1966 (Cask 487, 51.6%)						320	
Springbank Local Barley – 1966 (Cask 480, 54.4%)				200			
Springbank Local Barley – 1966 (Cask 488, 52.1%)					420		
Springbank Local Barley – 1966 (Cask 493, 56.8%)						360	
Springbank Local Barley – 1966 (Cask 500, 54.2%)						300	
Springbank Local Barley – 1966 (Cask 507, 55%)						340	
Springbank – 1966 (Cask 511, 55%)	90						

Left to right.
Springbank Local Barley – 1966,
Springbank – 33-year-old (Pear shaped)

Whisky Auction Sale Results (£s)	2000	2001	2002	2003	2004	2005	2006
Springbank – 1966 (Cask 473, 52.5%)	183						
Springbank – 1966 (Cask 474, 51.2%)	183						
Springbank – 1966 (Cask 475, 52%)	183						
Springbank – 1966 (Cask 486, 53%)		300					
Springbank – 1972 (Tesco, 70 cl., 46%)							190
Springbank – 1977 (Cadenhead's, 54.5%)					190		
Springbank – 1977 (Cadenhead's, 55.4%)							220
Springbank – 1978	75						
Springbank – 1979 (Cadenhead's, 53%)					145		
Springbank – 1979 (Open Golf, 1995)						170	
Springbank – 1979 (SMWS, 56.2%)					140		
Springbank – 1979 (SMWS, 56.9%)						60	
Springbank – 1980 (Cadenhead's, 58%)			115				
Springbank – 1980 (Cadenhead's, 56.7%)						130	
Springbank – 1980 (Cadenhead's, 56.6%)						175	
Springbank – 1989 (Cask 036)		220					
Springbank – 1989 (Whisky Castle, 46%)			65		40		
Springbank – 1991 (Murray McDavid, 46%)					40		
Springbank – 1993 (Signatory for Luvians signed box by Tiger Woods)		600					
Springbank – 1993 (Signatory for Luvians)			100–150				70

St. Magdalene

St. Magdalene has appeared at auction recently, bottlings by Gordon & MacPhail, Rare Malts and the Scotch Malt Whisky Society, the rarest bottling to date being the Centenary of United Distillers Engineering in Glasgow

Whisky Auction Sale Results (£s)	2000	2001	2002	2003	2004	2005	2006
St. Magdalene – 10-year-old – 1982 (Cadenhead's, 62.3%)							37
St. Magdalene – 12-year-old – 1982 (Cadenhead's, 63%)				47			170
St. Magdalene – 15-year-old – 1964 (Cadenhead's, 80 degrees)					190		
St. Magdalene – 16-year-old – 1963 (G & M)				130			
St. Magdalene – 18-year-old – 1964 (G & M)	57				60–67	100	
St. Magdalene – 19-year-old – 1979 (63.8%)						45–62	60

Left to right.
St. Magdalene – 20-year-old
(United Distillers Engineering),
St. Magdalene – 15-year-old
(Cadenhead's)

Whisky Auction Sale Results (£s)	2000	2001	2002	2003	2004	2005	2006
St. Magdalene – 20-year-old – 1978 (100 years of United Distillers Engineering, 62.7%)				500	420		380–390
St. Magdalene – 21-year-old – 1982 (Hart Bros, 56.5%)					37	20–23	
St. Magdalene – 24-year-old – 1964 (G & M)	60						
St. Magdalene – 23-year-old – 1970 (60.6%)			53				
St. Magdalene – 23-year-old – 1970 (58.1%)				72	65–83	62	100
St. Magdalene – 23-year-old – 1970 (58.43%)					75		
St. Magdalene – 25-year-old (Cadenhead's, 44.2%)							120
St. Magdalene – 30-year-old – 1964 (Cadenhead's, 48.5%)					120		120
St. Magdalene – 1964 (G & M)					50		80
St. Magdalene – 1965 (G & M)	46		45–70	62–80	31–57	90	70
St. Magdalene – 1966 (G & M, 70 cl.)	27		70		40–80	80	50
St. Magdalene – 1975 (SMWS, 64.6%)		167					
St. Magdalene – 1978 (SMWS, 64.1%)		189					110
St. Magdalene – 1980 (G & M Centenary)						60	70–75
St. Magdalene – 1981 (G & M)	28		37		40–42	60	
St. Magdalene – 1982 (G & M)				26			
St. Magdalene – 1982 (SMWS, 63.5%)			47				

Strathisla

Mature Strathisla bottled by Gordon & MacPhail and distillery anniversary bottlings have achieved the best auction results to date

Whisky Auction Sale Results (£s)	2000	2001	2002	2003	2004	2005	2006
Strathisla – 8-year-old (75 cl.)		130	47	35	60		60
Strathisla – 10-year-old (26 2/3 fl. ozs., 70 proof)						200	130
Strathisla – 12-year-old (75 cl.)				40	70		43–47
Strathisla – 12-year-old (75 cl. label printed in script)					280		
Strathisla – 15-year-old (G & M, 75 cl.)			33–73		33–60	33–52	
Strathisla – 15-year-old (G & M, Securo screw cap)			170				
Strathisla – 15-year-old (26 2/3 fl. oz)				90–95		90	
Strathisla – 21-year-old (G & M, 75 cl.)				40			50
Strathisla – 24-year-old – 1979 (First Cask)							40
Strathisla – 24-year-old – 1960 (G & M, crystal decanter)	260		160				
Strathisla Bicentenary – 25-year-old (Magnum)	860						
Strathisla – 25-year-old (Restoration Anniversary)	200	190	110–120	100–190		100–110	90–130
Strathisla – 25-year-old (G & M, Queen's Silver Jubilee, 1977)					145		
Strathisla – 27-year-old – 1976 (Cooper's Choice, 46%)							33
Strathisla – 27-year-old – 1976 (Mission Selection 2, 46%)							42
Strathisla – 30-year-old (G & M)	60			70	45–55		
Strathisla – 34-year-old – 1967 (Hart Bros, 46%)			40	53	47	50	40–57
Strathisla – 35-year-old – 1967 (Peerless, 48.8%)					70		
Strathisla Bicentenary – 35-year-old		280–290			320	205–220	230
Strathisla Bicentenary – 35-year-old (With plate)		520	280–400		260		220

Whisky Auction Sale Results (£s)	2000	2001	2002	2003	2004	2005	2006
Strathisla – 35-year-old (G & M)		80		70			100
Strathisla – 40-year-old (Crystal decanter)	230						
Strathisla – 1937 (G & M, label discoloured)	125					140	
Strathisla – 1937 (G & M)	200	180	180				
Strathisla – 34-year-old – 1937 (G & M)	310						
Strathisla – 35-year-old – 1937 (G & M)	300						
Strathisla – 40-year-old – 1948 (Glass decanter)	260	240					
Strathisla – 1949 (Captain Burns)			105				
Strathisla – 47-year-old – 1937 (G & M)		230		210		200	
Strathisla Royal Wedding (1948 and 1961)				95			
Strathisla – 1949 (G & M)					130		
Strathisla – 1953 (G & M)			250				
Strathisla – 1954 (G & M)						140	
Strathisla – 1955 (G & M)	50–125				90		
Strathisla – 1970 (G & M)			60	25			
Strathisla – 1974 (SMWS, 57.9%)		189					

Strathisla – 25-year-old – Restoration of Distillery

Strathmill

This 1930s replica bottling and Limited Edition Centenary bottling have fetched respectable prices at auction together with other expressions of Strathmill sold at auction in recent years

Whisky Auction Sale Results (£s)	2000	2001	2002	2003	2004	2005	2006
Strathmill Fine Old Replica		370–420			520	460–500	
Strathmill Centenary (1891–1991, 100 bottles)				850–900	680		
Strathmill – 10-year-old (Friar John Cor, 43%)			65		30		
Strathmill – 10-year-old (Scottish Wildlife)			42				42–47
Strathmill – 10-year-old (MWBH bonding, 59.4%)			75				
Strathmill – 11-year-old – 1980 (Cadenhead's, 60.6%)			27	35	135		110
Strathmill – 11-year-old – 1985 (Signatory, 43%)					43–45		
Strathmill – 15-year-old (Manager's Dram, released 2003)					95–100	98	100–130
Strathmill – 15-year-old (Flora & Fauna)							25
Strathmill – 26-year-old – 1974 (First Cask)					40–50		
Strathmill – 1980 (Cadenhead's, 60.5%)					70–140		
Strathmill – 1980 (SMWS, 60.7%)			147		80	130	
Strathmill – 1991 (G & M)							37

Left to right.
Strathmill Centenary,
Strathmill Fine Old Replica

Stromness

This is the only historical example of a bottle from Stromness Distillery to appear at auction over the last decade

Whisky Auction Sale Results (£s)	2000	2001	2002	2003	2004	2005	2006
Old Orkney Real Liqueur – Early 20th century	3200						

Talisker

Mature Talisker bottled by Gordon & MacPhail, rare old expressions and distillery bottlings have fetched some respectable prices at auction to date

Whisky Auction Sale Results (£s)	2000	2001	2002	2003	2004	2005	2006
Talisker – Believed Mid-19th century		3900					
Talisker Real Old (John Haig & Co)		3500					
Finest Old Vatted Talisker – Believed early 20th century (C J Melrose & Co, York, driven cork)			1700				
Talisker (USA import, stopper cork)	580						780
Talisker (G & M, 100 degrees)	50						
Talisker (G & M, 80 degrees)				200			
Talisker 175th Anniversary (45.8%)							55
Talisker Limited Edition (Distillery, 59.2%)					40	30	
Talisker Limited Edition (Distillery, 60%)					40	45	
Talisker Limited Edition (Isle of Eigg Trust, 60%)		300	195		110	140–210	130–170
Talisker – 8-year-old (Distillers Agency, 45.8%)	60–240		340		150–230	340	
Talisker – 8-year-old (J Walker & Sons, 45.8%)			270	185–220	215		
Talisker – 8-year-old (Distillers Agency, 80 degrees)				65–220	220		
Talisker – Over 8-year-old (Distillery, 80 degrees)				260			
Talisker – Over 8-year-old (G & M, 80 degrees)				170			
Talisker – 10-year-old – 1989 (59.3%)			75				
Talisker – 12-year-old (Distillers Agency, 43%)		170		240		210	
Talisker – 12-year-old (J Walker & Sons, 43%)		180			135		
Talisker – 12-year-old (USA import, spring cap)		1500					
Talisker – 16-year-old – 1979 (Cadenhead's, 63.2%)					52		

Whisky Auction Sale Results (£s)	2000	2001	2002	2003	2004	2005	2006
Talisker – 1934 (Berry Bros & Rudd)		320					
Talisker – 1947 (G & M, 40%)	210–250	220				265	
Talisker – 1952 (G & M, 40%)						205	
Talisker – 1953 (G & M, 40%)				190	240	240	
Talisker – 1954 (G & M, 40%)				190	240		
Talisker – 1955 (G & M, 52.9%)		250			220–260		
Talisker – 1955 (G & M, 50.4%)					150		
Talisker – 1955 (G & M, 53.6%)					230–250		270
Talisker – 1956 (G & M, 54.4%)			180–200	180–230			290
Talisker – 1956 (G & M, 70 degrees)			170		260	210–255	

Left to right.
Talisker (Melrose's),
Talisker – 25-year-old,
Talisker Isle of Eigg Heritage Trust

Whisky Auction Sale Results (£s)	2000	2001	2002	2003	2004	2005	2006
Talisker – 1957 (G & M, 100 degrees)				240–260			360–380
Talisker – 1957 (G & M, 51.1%)			170–190	190–220			
Talisker – 1957 (G & M, 51.9%)			145–210				
Talisker – 1957 (G & M, 53.3%)				190	170		
Talisker – 1958 (G & M, 40%)			160		170–230		
Talisker – 20-year-old – 1957 (Cadenhead's)		170					
Talisker – 20-year-old – 1981 (62%)						52–85	55–90
Talisker – 20-year-old – 1982 (58.8%)						40–45	
Talisker – 21-year-old – 1957 (Cadenhead's)			82				
Talisker – 21-year-old – 1951 (G & M)	210–280	240–320					300

Left to right.
Talsker – Over 8-year-old,
Talisker – 12-year-old,
Talisker – 1967

Whisky Auction Sale Results (£s)	2000	2001	2002	2003	2004	2005	2006
Talisker – 21-year-old – 1952 (G & M)	200						
Talisker – 24-year-old – 1953 (G & M)	220						220
Talisker – 35-year-old – 1947 (G & M)		170					
Talisker – 37-year-old – 1955 (G & M, 50.4%)		310					
Talisker – 1967 (G & M, 100 degrees)			110				
Talisker – 1969 (G & M, 80 degrees)			150				
Talisker – 1970 (G & M, 52.2%)					130		
Talisker – 1972 (G & M, 100 degrees)					195	130	
Talisker – 25-year-old – 1975 (55%)							90
Talisker – 25-year-old – 1975 (59.9%)					110		80
Talisker – 28-year-old – 1973 (Cask 4633, 43.3%)				400–570		400–500	820
Talisker – 1974 (Private bottling)			65				
Talisker – 1976 (SMWS, 64.5%)							160
Talisker – 1979 (SMWS, 64.3%)		67					
Talisker – 1979 (Cadenhead's, 64%)						95	
Talisker – 1986 (45.8%)				45	34	28–35	
Talisker – 1988 (43%)						52	
Talisker Limited Edition – 1989 (59.3%)				55		45	27
Talisker – 1991 (Double matured)							25
Talikser – 1992 (Double matured)							32

Tamdhu

Many mature and old expressions of Tamdhu have appeared at auction recently

Whisky Auction Sale Results (£s)	2000	2001	2002	2003	2004	2005	2006
Tamdhu Reserve – 1900 (R H Thomson & Co)	1450						
Tamdhu (Calvert UK, 26 2/3 fl. oz, 70 degrees)			90				
Tamdhu (Cadenhead's, stopper cork, 80 degrees)				190			
Tamdhu – 1920 (Matthew Gloag & Son)	400						
Tamdhu – 8-year-old (26 2/3 fl. oz, 70 degrees)			90		140–200		
Tamdhu – 10-year-old (75 cl.)		62		31	30–60		37
Tamdhu – 10-year-old – 1990 (Hart Bros)		27					
Tamdhu – 15-year-old (75 cl.)					26		
Tamdhu – 15-year-old (Decanter, 75 cl.)		60	65	73	37–55		
Tamdhu – 15-year-old – 1985 (Adelphi, 55.3%)							20
Tamdhu – 17-year-old (Cadenhead's, 80 degrees)					90		
Tamdhu – Glenlivet – 22-year-old (J Bradley)	190						
Tamdhu – 23-year-old – 1950 (Highland Distilleries)		160	210				
Tamdhu – 1957 (G & M, 40%)					100		
Tamdhu – 1960 (G & M. 40%)					52		
Tamdhu – 27-year-old – 1970 (Signatory, 49.5%)		75					
Tamdhu – Glenlivet – 30-year-old – 1963 (Cadenhead's, 48.2%)					60		
Tamdhu – 33-year-old – 1969 (Hart Bros, 40.5%)					37	35	37–50
Tamdhu – 42-year-old – 1958 (Hart Bros, 40.8%)	115–260	80–160	70–100	70–90	60–82	50–80	80–90

Tamnavulin

This small and varied selection of expressions of Tamnavulin have appeared at auction recently

Whisky Auction Sale Results (£s)	2000	2001	2002	2003	2004	2005	2006
Tamnavulin – Glenlivet (Cylindrical bottle)			37				
Tamnavulin – Glenlivet (26 2/3 fl. oz, 75 degrees)			60			45–50	50
Tamnavulin – Stillman's Dram – 1968	35	45	30	25	58	55	100
Tamnavulin – The Old Mill – 1968		45	40	40	57–80		
Tamnavulin – Stillman's Dram – 1970			30–45		57	55	
Tamnavulin – 1978 (Blackadder, 60.2%)					38		
Tamnavulin – Stillman's Dram – 21-year-old (45%)						57	
Tamnavulin – Stillman's Dram – 24-year-old (45%)			27			45	32–42
Tamnavulin – Stillman's Dram – 25-year-old (45%)	30	45	40			35–60	
Tamnavulin New Century – 25-year-old – 1974 (45%)						40–60	
Tamnavulin – 25-year-old – 1977 (First Cask)							39
Tamnavulin – Stillman's Dram – 27-year-old (45%)					75		42–60
Tamnavulin – Stillman's Dram – 28-year-old (45%)						40	
Tamnavulin – Stillman's Dram – 29-year-old (45%)					60–140	35–82	
Tamnavulin – Stillman's Dram – 30-year-old (45%)							60
Tamnavulin – Glenlivet – 8-year-old (75 cl.)		70	40		116		24–35
Tamnavulin – Glenlivet – 10-year-old (70 cl.)			30	40		45	
Tamnavulin – Glenlivet – 10-year-old (75 cl.)					33		
Tamnavulin – Glenlivet – 10-year-old (Decanter, 75 cl.)					30	23	

Whisky Auction Sale Results (&s)	2000	2001	2002	2003	2004	2005	2006
Tamnavulin – 10-year-old (70 cl.)			30				
Tamnavulin – 14-year-old (53.2%)		180					

Teaninich

This small and interesting selection of Teaninich has been sold successfully at auction recently

Whisky Auction Sale Results (£s)	2000	2001	2002	2003	2004	2005	2006
Teaninich – 10-year-old (Flora & Fauna)			22	26	27–48		25–52
Teaninich – 12-year-old (Re-opening, 1991)			260				
Teaninich – 15-year-old – 1968 (G & M)			65				
Teaninich – 15-year-old – 1969 (G & M)							120
Teaninich – 15-year-old – 1971 (G & M)						80	
Teaninich – 16-year-old – 1981 (First Cask)		20			36	20	
Teaninich – 17-year-old (Manager's Dram)			50–80	77	70–130	60–80	77–85
Teaninich – 22-year-old (R W Duthie, 46%)				120			
Teaninich – 22-year-old – 1957 (Cadenhead's, 45.7%)	95		145	.	110	85	160
Teaninich – 23-year-old – 1972 (64.95%)		57			63–90	55–77	50–90
Teaninich – 23-year-old – 1973 (57.1%)		47			60		57–72
Teaninich – 24-year-old – 1973 (Adelphi, 56.6%)		35					50
Teaninich – 24-year-old – 1975 (Hart Bros, 43%)					25–40		
Teaninich – 24-year-old – 1976 (Hart Bros, 43%)						30	27
Teaninich – 26-year-old – 1957 (Cadenhead's, 46%)					130		
Teaninich – 26-year-old – 1973 (Douglas Laing, 50%)					23		
Teaninich – 1972 (G & M)						38	
Teaninich – 1975 (G & M)			24	23	30–40	26	22
Teaninich – 1976 (G & M)							32
Teaninich – 1980 (SMWS, 66.1%)					120		

Whisky Auction Sale Results (£s)	2000	2001	2002	2003	2004	2005	2006
Teaninich – 1982 (G & M)			40–60		40		
Teaninich – 1983 (SMWS, 53.6%)			47				
Teaninich – 1983 (G & M)						47	

Teaninich – 15-year-old
(G & M)

Tomatin – 23-year-old
(Cadenhead's)

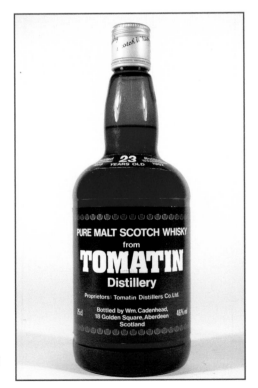

Tomatin

This small selection of expressions of Tomatin have appeared at auction in recent years

Whisky Auction Sale Results (£s)	2000	2001	2002	2003	2004	2005	2006
Tomatin – 5-year-old (75 cl.)		70					
Tomatin – 10-year-old (75 cl.)			25–23	20–38	20–42		
Tomatin – 10-year-old (26 2/3 fl. oz)			53	30	60–67		
Tomatin – 15-year-old (Crystal decanter)	170						
Tomatin – 15-year-old – 1964 (G & M)				90			
Tomatin – 15-year-old – 1970 (G & M)			90				
Tomatin – 18-year-old – 1976 (Signatory, 43%)			28				
Tomatin – 18-year-old – 1976 (First Cask)			37		32	30	40
Tomatin – 23-year-old – 1958 (Cadenhead's, 46%)					95		
Tomatin – 23-year-old – 1966 (Signatory, 46%)	62						37
Tomatin – 25-year-old – 1966		70–80	65	85	110	70–80	
Tomatin Centenary – 30-year-old				80	120–130	110	150–160
Tomatin – 33-year-old – 1967 (Milroy's, 53.3%)		100					
Tomatin – 37-year-old – 1965 (Hart Bros, 47.2%)					27–30	45	37
Tomatin – 40-year-old – 1962 (Douglas Laing, 44%)					60	60–130	85–130
Tomatin – 1963 (Private bottling)			65				
Tomatin – 1964 (Spirit of Scotland)			90	60–70	52–58	60	
Tomatin – 1968 (G & M)	39					37	
Tomatin – 1974 (1494–1994)	30						
Tomatin – 1976 (Cadenhead's, 58.6%)				40			
Tomatin – 1978 (SMWS, 57.4%)					55		45

Tomintoul

Only this small selection of expressions of Tomintoul have been sold with success at auction recently

Whisky Auction Sale Results (£s)	2000	2001	2002	2003	2004	2005	2006
Tomintoul – Glenlivet (Cylindrical bottle)			20–37		30–47	37–63	23–30
Tomintoul – Glenlivet – 8-year-old (Whyte & MacKay, 75 cl.)				31–60	62		
Tomintoul – Glenlivet – 12-year-old (Whyte & MacKay, 75 cl.)					26–37		
Tomintoul – Glenlivet – 12-year-old – 1965				27			
Tomintoul – 17-year-old – 1976 (Signatory)			28				
Tomintoul – Glenlivet – 18-year-old – 1967 (ABC Ltd)				40			
Tomintoul – 18-year-old – 1976 (First Cask)			20				
Tomintoul – 18-year-old – 1971 (Prestonfield House)		115					
Tomintoul – 23-year-old – 1976 (Adelphi, 54.3%)						20	22
Tomintoul – 30-year-old – 1966 (Signatory, 52.7%)			72				
Tomintoul – 31-year-old – 1973 (Mission Selection 4, 46%)							40
Tomintoul – Stillman's Dram – 1966 (45%)						63	
Tomintoul – 34-year-old – 1966 (Adelphi, 52.1%)							73
Tomintoul – 34-year-old – 1966 (Milroy's, 49.01%)		93–105					
Tomintoul – 35-year-old – 1966 (Signatory, 46.1%)					90		
Tomintoul – 1976 (SMWS, 63.5%)			47				

Tormore

These are the only examples of Tormore that have appeared at auction recently

Whisky Auction Sale Results (£s)	2000	2001	2002	2003	2004	2005	2006
Tormore (Long John Distillery Ltd)			50				
Tormore – Glenlivet – 5-year-old (75 cl.)		80				90	
Tormore – 10-year-old (Long John Distillery Ltd)	60		50	31–65	33–85	90	
Tormore – 10-year-old (75 cl.)						90–140	85–120
Tormore – 15-year-old (Allied)				32	20–30	18–27	

Tullibardine

This small selection of Tullibardine has been sold with success at auction recently

Whisky Auction Sale Results (£s)	2000	2001	2002	2003	2004	2005	2006
Tullibardine – 5-year-old (Italian import, 70 degrees)		55	77				
Tullibardine – 10-year-old (Italian import)		70		31			
Tullibardine – 10-year-old (26 2/3 fl. oz)			55	53	37–45		30–35
Tullibardine – 13-year-old – 1965 (Cadenhead's, 45.7%)					80		
Tullibardine – 1987 (46%)							40
Tullibardine – 15-year-old – 1989 (Hart Bros, 49.8%)						21	20
Tullibardine – 16-year-old – 1961 (Cadenhead's, 45.7%)						140	
Tullibardine – 1964 (44.6%)							160–170
Tullibardine – 22-year-old – 1972 (Signatory, 53.5%)						50	
Tullibardine – Stillman's Dram – 25-year-old (45%)	32–45		40		35–45	45	
Tullibardine – Stillman's Dram – 30-year-old (45%)					55–60	40–45	60
Tullibardine – 35-year-old – 1966 (Adelphi, 54.6%)							50
Tullibardine – Vintage 1993					28		

COLLECTING MALT WHISKY

NORTHERN IRELAND

Coleraine

This fine malt from Coleraine distillery is very rare now, this was the last cask bottled

Whiskey Auction Sale Results (£s)	2000	2001	2002	2003	2004	2005	2006
Coleraine – 34-year-old – 1959 (57.1%)	550	600		700		700	650

Coleraine-34 year-old

Jameson's

Although this is a small selection of Jameson's that have been sold with success at auction recently, the healthy results show the popularity among collectors

Whiskey Auction Sale Results (£s)	2000	2001	2002	2003	2004	2005	2006
John Jameson's Old Whiskey – Distilled 1880					350		
John Jameson & Son – 1912 (Berry Bros, poor label)					200		
Jameson's – Early 20th Century		400–440					
Jameson's Dublin Whiskey – Circa 1950			250				
JJ12 (75 cl.)			65				
Jameson's Liqueur Dublin Whiskey			65				
Jameson's – 7-year-old		200					
Jameson's Dublin Whiskey – 7-year-old – Circa 1940				350			
Jameson's 15-year-old (26 2/3 fl. oz)					180	165	
Jameson's Bow Street – 27-year-old (Cadenhead's, 68.2%)					230		
Jameson's Bow Street – 27-year-old – 1963 (Cadenhead's 68.1%)				150			
Jameson's – 37-year-old – 1949 (Avery's)		250–350	280–360				

Jameson's – Early 20th Century

Old Comber

This fine malt from Comber distillery is very rare now, production ceased in the 1950s

Whiskey Auction Sale Results (£s)	2000	2001	2002	2003	2004	2005	2006
Comber Pure Pot Still (Half, purchased 1950)			90				
Old Comber – 30-year-old	210	270	140–170	160–170			

Midleton

This is a small but select range of Midleton that has been sold with success at auction recently

Whiskey Auction Sale Results (£s)	2000	2001	2002	2003	2004	2005	2006
Midleton Very Rare – Bottled 1984		90	55–70		55		120
Midleton Very Rare – Bottled 1985			65				
Midleton Very Rare – Bottled 1988							180
Midleton Very Rare – Bottled 1998	25						
Midleton Very Rare – Bottled 1992		90					
Midleton Very Rare – Bottled 1994		90	45				
Midleton Very Rare – Bottled 2001							70
Midleton Very Rare – Bottled 2002							80
Midleton – 25-year-old (43%)					220		
Midleton – 30-year-old – 1969 (40%)						430	